DEDICATION

I heard a sermon one day by Chuck Swindoll where he spoke on the topic of "A Turtle on a Fence Post." His point was that if you're driving down the road and you see a turtle on a fence post, chances are he didn't get there by himself! I remember thinking the story was both funny and poignant; in a lot of ways I represent that turtle. Any of the success I have attained—any of the positions I have gained—is attributable to the people around me. My place in the world is a brighter place thanks to my family, my friends, and my co-workers.

YOUR PLACE IN THIS WORLD

DISCOVERING GOD'S WILL FOR THE LIFE IN FRONT OF YOU

MICHAEL W. SMITH

WITH

MICHAEL NOLAN

THOMAS NELSON PUBLISHERS
Nashville

Published in Nashville, Tennessee, by Thomas Nelson, Inc., Publishers.

Scripture quotations noted NKJV are from THE NEW KING JAMES VERSION. Copyright © 1979, 1980, 1982, 1990, Thomas Nelson, Inc., Publishers.

Scripture quotations noted CEV are from THE COMTEMPORARY ENGLISH VERSION. © 1991 by the American Bible Society. Used by permission.

Scripture quotations noted The Message are from *The Message: The New Testament in Contemporary English*. Copyright © 1993 by Eugene H. Peterson.

Scripture quotations noted NASB are from the NEW AMERICAN STANDARD BIBLE®, © Copyright The Lockman Foundation 1960, 1962, 1963, 1968, 1971, 1972, 1973, 1975, 1977 Used by permission.

Scripture quotations noted NIV are from the HOLY BIBLE: NEW INTERNA-TIONAL VERSION®. Copyright © 1973, 1978, 1984, by International Bible Society. Used by permission of Zondervan Publishing House. All rights reserved.

Scripture quotations noted NLT are from the *Holy Bible*, New Living Translation, copyright © 1996. Used by permission of Tyndale House Publishers, Inc., Wheaton, Illinois 60189. All rights reserved.

Scripture quotations noted TLB are from *The Living Bible*, copyright © 1971. Used by permission of Tyndale House Publishers, Inc., Wheaton, Illinois 60189. All rights reserved.

Library of Congress Cataloging-in-Publication Data

Your Place in this world : discovering God's will for the life in front of you / Michael W. Smith with Michael Nolan.
   p.   cm.
Includes bibliographical references.
ISBN 0-7852-7020-5
1. Youth—Religious life.   I. Nolan, Mike, 1957– .   II. Title.
BV4531.2.S594   1998
248.8'3—dc21

98-44540
CIP

Printed in the United States of America.
1 2 3 4 5 6 QPH 03 02 01 00 99 98

CONTENTS

Welcome to Your Life: An Introduction vii

Part 1: Place

1. Place in This World 3

2. All the Wrong Places 13

3. A Place to Belong 20

4. A Place to Grow 36

5. A Place to Make a Difference 46

6. A Place to Start 56

Part 2: Purpose

7. The Purpose of Purpose 71

8. Our Not-So-Secret Ambition 83

9. Unexpected Paths 94

10. Finding Your Purpose 105

Part 3: Passion

11. Holy Fire   115

12. Focus of the Flame   123

13. The Great and the Hardly Noticeable   134

14. Rekindling the Flame   143

15. Keep the Flame Burning   150

Part 4: God's Plan

16. Distant Drums   161

17. The Big Picture and the Little Details   169

18. Wanting, Worrying, and Waiting   179

19. Pursuit of the Dream   189

20. Plan B and Beyond   197

21. Your Place in This World   205

     Notes   213

Welcome to Your Life

An Introduction

ou are here."

Ever seen those three words boldly printed on a map marked with an arrow? Perhaps you were trying to navigate from one airport concourse to another. Maybe you were looking for the easiest way to get across a university campus. Or you were visiting a mall and needed a little help finding a certain store.

It's reassuring to encounter one of those maps because it leaves nothing to interpretation. "You are here." You locate where you want to go and then plot a path to get there. Sounds simple—and sometimes it actually is.

Our lives are not so cut-and-dried. Practically

every person I've ever known has come to an uncomfortable point in life where he or she feels lost. Questions arise. Where am I? How did I get here? Where am I going?

For some, this confusion is an occasional occurrence. For others, it seems more like a way of life. My hope is that this book puts some markers on your map, clarifies what you're looking for, and gives you the guidance you need to truly find your place in this world.

Hard times and hard answers bring growth. Unfortunately, growing can be a slow process. But the result is far beyond what you could ever achieve on your own. Romans 5:3–5 tells us to rejoice "in tribulations, knowing that tribulation produces perseverance; and perseverance, character; and character, hope. Now hope does not disappoint, because the love of God has been poured out in our hearts by the Holy Spirit who was given to us" (NKJV).

I invite you to embark with me on a journey of the heart. If you choose to come along, I believe the Holy Spirit will reveal some things about who you are and who you're becoming. I encourage you to be ready to give as well as receive.

The book is divided into four main sections: Place, Purpose, Passion, and God's Plan. Place is your spiritual and emotional launching pad, a "home" for support and encouragement, something we long for and need to provide for others. Purpose is where we're going with our lives, our mission, the reason we're here. Passion is the energy that propels us forward, the fire inside that keeps us fully alive instead of merely existing. God's Plan is a look at our journey so far, as well as a glimpse at what the Lord may have for us in the future.

Blessings in Christ,

PART I

PLACE

A "home" for support
and encouragement—
something we both long for
and provide for others

ONE

PLACE IN THIS WORLD

etters. Through the years, the mailbox has been an unfailing source of inspiration. The letters I receive let me know what people are thinking about my music and often provide direction when it's time to work on new material.

Just as all of the songs on my *Big Picture* album were in some way born from the mail I receive, "Place in This World" was inspired from things people were telling me, letters like these:

> Dear Michael,
> I don't know where my life is going. It seems like everything and everybody is messed up.
>
> JASON, AGE 17

Dear Michael,
I became a Christian last year and
thought that suddenly I would finally feel
like I had found a place to fit but that
hasn't happened yet.

KARA, AGE 15

Dear Michael,
I don't know if you get many letters from
people my age but, after listening to your
songs, I feel like you would understand. I
can't believe that I've gotten to this point
in life but still don't seem to have any
direction. It seems like I just drift from
one relationship to the next, from job to
job, and church to church.

ANDREA, AGE 28

Although the ages vary and the situations may
be quite different, it seems that vast numbers of people struggle to find a place where they feel welcome,
a purpose that gives meaning to life, a passion that
energizes them to move forward, and a confidence
that God really does have a plan for their lives.

Sometime in 1989, Wayne Kirkpatrick and I got together to work on songs for my next record. I sat down at the piano in my studio and played a melody I had begun. He was thumbing through his notebook where he jots down all his ideas for lyrics and titles, looking for something that might fit with the music. When he came across the phrase *place in this world*, the two seemed to click.

Wayne wrote the chorus, then called Amy Grant to enlist her help. They met at her house and spent hours reminiscing about their high school years. Both had been quiet, insecure, really questioning whether anybody truly liked them.

By this time, I had created a music track, which they played as they worked on verses that portrayed the feelings familiar to most people. The words were simple, but they rang true.

I never considered whether or not the words had crossover potential. In fact, quite the opposite. My manager and friend Michael Blanton had said early on that we should focus on our core audience. "On the last album, we recorded a few songs we thought might become pop hits but nothing happened, so let's just let that go," Michael said.

"Instead, let's keep this album aimed straight at the Christian market, totally focused on Smitty fans."

Wayne speculated that could be one reason God chose to use the song as He did—our motives were completely pure. We weren't trying to appeal to the pop and Christian marketplaces simultaneously. We weren't being vague to gain the acceptance of skeptical pop radio program directors. We were just doing our best to deliver this simple message: God knows what you're going through, and He won't leave you.

When we finished recording the song, I was pleased with what we had created but I had no idea what would become of it. I was just excited that this new song was a solid response of hope to many of the people who were writing me.

THE HAND OF PROVIDENCE

About a year before "Place in This World" was written, Reunion Records, my record label, had entered into an agreement with the mainstream Geffen label to introduce songs to pop radio. Claire Parr, Geffen director of adult music promotion and marketing, was a Christian but knew very little about Christian music.

At the time *Go West, Young Man* was scheduled to be released, her plate was already full with huge projects from well-known artists. As she listened to a stack of CDs she had received, "Place in This World" immediately caught her attention, and she told her boss she thought it had great potential.

Geffen was uncertain that it wanted to put much effort into it, but Claire literally put her job on the line to promote it. She found few allies in her fight until all of the Geffen executives came to see one of my shows at Universal Amphitheatre in Los Angeles. The concert and the music was so different from what they were expecting, many changed their attitude.

The song was released to pop radio in early 1990, but little happened. Claire had never encountered the phrase "spiritual warfare" but she found herself right in the middle of a battle. She remembered, "During that time there were health problems, meetings that went really badly, all kinds of things that could have killed the record. But there was also so much prayer from so many people."

She and her staff worked on "Place in This World" for six months to make it a hit. Two DJs in Cincinnati and one in San Diego took a risk by playing the song early on and were instrumental in giving the song momentum.

Every time the song slipped on the charts, a new opportunity came along. We'd fall back a few notches, then *People* magazine would want to do a story or *Regis and Kathie Lee* would invite me to do their show.

I never knew who would be supportive or who would hate my guts. I even experienced a backlash among Christians who questioned whether I had "sold out" my faith by pursuing pop exposure.

After much hard work by Claire and her staff, the song rose to number seven on the Billboard Hot 100 and number four on adult contemporary charts. It was an achievement I had barely believed possible.

Why was "Place in This World" so successful? I think God wanted to use that song to speak truth to a lot of hearts, especially to people who had never heard of me and probably would never have listened to Christian radio. Thousands, maybe millions, of people know all too well the feelings the song expressed:

> *A heart that's hopeful*
> *A head that's full of dreams*
> *But this becoming*
> *Is harder than it seems*
> *Looking for a reason*
> *Roaming through the night to find*
>
> *My place in this world*
> *My place in this world*
> *Not a lot to lean on*
> *I need your light to help me to find*
> *My place in this world*
> *My place in this world*

The initial response from Christians was strong but the pop radio exposure took this song about God to levels beyond my wildest dreams. As letters began to roll in, I realized I had truly bridged the gap to deliver a message that touched people who were not following Jesus. The lyrics of the second verse reached them in their questions:

If there are millions
Down on their knees
Among the many
Can you still hear me
Hear me asking
Where do I belong
Is there a vision
That I can call my own[1]

In the months that followed the release of "Place in This World," I was repeatedly humbled to learn what God had done in people's lives with that song. Marriages were healed, families began to mend, and people who were planning to kill themselves sought help instead of ending their lives.

Jesus told a parable about a tiny mustard seed being planted and becoming a tree large enough to be a sanctuary for birds to rest (Mark 4:30–32). In its own God-ordained way, "Place in This World" had grown to become a sanctuary for people to take a moment, reflect upon what was going on in their lives, and focus their attention on God.

THE SONG GOES ON

I recently visited Christian bookstores in five cities on a single day as part of a promotional tour. In each place, at least one person walked up to me and said something like "That song saved my life" and then walked away. No details, no explanations.

I know from reading my mail what kinds of possibilities existed. Loneliness. Depression. Despair. Anger. Meaninglessness. Worthlessness. All kinds of abuse.

It's said that a candle appears brighter if you place it in a truly dark place. Evidently, that's what God has done over and over again with that song. It's like the picture presented in Isaiah 9:2: "The people who walked in darkness / Have seen a great light; / Those who dwelt in the land of the shadow of death, / Upon them a light has shined" (NKJV). God found people in dark places and put "Place in This World" in their path.

As I think about its meaning, I don't belive that place is merely a sanctuary from the storms of life. It can be a hospital to recuperate and heal from life's tragedies, a boot camp to prepare for what lies ahead, and a launching pad for a great future.

As we will learn in the next chapter, the first consideration in being in the right place is to not be in the wrong place.

TWO

ALL THE
WRONG PLACES

ver gone into a grocery when you're hungry? You wander up and down the aisles, a bit overwhelmed by all you see. With a gnawing in your stomach, almost everything looks good. You gravitate toward items you can chow down on before you even get to the parking lot. Unless you're really disciplined (or you know how little is in your wallet), you'll load your cart with chips, cookies, candy, and crackers. I picture my cart loaded with Milky Ways and M&Ms.

All of us were born with a tremendous appetite for love, a heart hungry for relationships. Just like that frantic run through the grocery, we may be tempted to grab whatever promises to satisfy us immediately. Little thought is given to consequences.

Deep down you know that your body will receive far more benefit if you shop carefully, buy healthy foods, go home, and take the time to prepare a complete meal. Eating right will give you the energy you need to keep going.

Contrast that to wolfing down a couple of candy bars as quickly as you can. You get little nutrition, a sugar buzz destined to send you crashing quickly, and nothing that will provide long-term nourishment. In fact, you'll probably be hungry again before long.

It's sad to realize how many people try to satisfy their souls with emotional "junk food." They fill up on all sorts of things that aren't good for them. A guy goes deeply in debt to finance a hot new sports car that he believes will impress people. A year later the car manufacturer will roll a new model off the assembly line, leaving that guy with a used car that isn't quite as cool as it was twelve months ago.

A girl can't stand the silence of her room so she stays on the move all the time—shopping, parties, school events. She feeds on the busyness because she can't bear the thought of letting her guard down long enough to reflect on her life.

A teenager plagued by awkwardness in social situations hops into an Internet chat room where he can pretend to be anyone he chooses. It's a feeling of freedom and power but there's a problem—no one is any closer to knowing who he really is, only the character he creates.

Maybe you can't relate to any of those scenarios, but I bet there's an example you could give from your own life.

Just as the grocery aisles are lined with all kinds of foods, there are multitudes of ways to stave off emotional hunger. Some people drink or get high. Some use sex. Others buy into the shallow promises of materialism. You can do it with sports or entertainment or work. You can even do it by misusing your faith, building a spiritual fortress that makes you rigid and rule oriented instead of sensitive to the leading of the Holy Spirit.

All of these things are, in a figurative sense, the object of our eating disorders. We can feed on them instead of turning to the real nourishment that comes from a true connection with God and honest relationships with others. The prophet Isaiah spoke of this problem 2,700 years ago:

If you are thirsty, come and drink water!
If you don't have any money, come, eat
  what you want!
  Drink wine and milk without paying
    a cent.
Why waste your money on what really
  isn't food?
  Why work hard for something that
    doesn't satisfy?
Listen carefully to me,
  and you will enjoy the very best foods.
  (55:1–2, CEV)

We have this marvelous promise, yet we waste our time on foods that don't really satisfy. They almost always damage our souls and lead us further from God.

CRY FOR LOVE

My friend Luci Freed has seen thousands of women who have made wrong choices. As director of Nashville's Crisis Pregnancy Support Center, she and her staff constantly meet girls and young women looking for love in all the wrong places.

"The vast majority of them got into a sexual situation because they were really lacking love from their fathers," she said. "I can't tell you how many times that's been at the root of an unplanned pregnancy. Most of these women don't even realize what their hunger was about until we've spent some time really going deeper into their situations."

Angie didn't get a lot of genuine affection from her dad. He kidded with her and occasionally hugged her, but he never really let her know that she was a lovely young woman, worthy of being honored and respected. At seventeen, she began hanging out with a guy who dealt drugs to make a living. He gave her pot in exchange for sex. It never occurred to her that she deserved better than the sad bartering arrangement she had agreed to.

As you can probably guess, she became pregnant. With help from Luci and others at the center, Angie began to see herself in a whole new way. By the time her baby was born, God had done some serious work in her family to improve and restore relationships.

BAD IDEAS

As if untangling the confusion of our hearts isn't hard enough, our culture convinces us that we are completely capable of satisfying ourselves. Media deliver these messages loud and clear: Only you can change your life. You're more important than others. Do what makes you feel better quickly.

It doesn't take a genius to see how enthusiastically our culture is chowing down on its diet of instant gratification, self-fulfillment, and temporary solutions. There is, however, a far better alternative.

SIT DOWN TO A FEAST

Have you ever been to the home of a great cook who is hard at work in her kitchen? Surely you were irresistibly drawn to the kitchen where you could smell bread baking and watch as pots of steaming food were carefully seasoned. Maybe it was a festive occasion like Thanksgiving or Christmas where every counter was covered with something good to eat. Those candy bars that seemed so appealing in the grocery would pale in comparison.

Just as a good meal takes time to prepare, the development of rich relationships with God and others takes time. But the rewards are just as satisfying. While our society races along at a frantic pace, the Lord whispers, "Be still, and know that I am God" (Ps. 46:10 NKJV).

But I don't have time to be still, we think. Yet, when we force ourselves to slow down and consider God, we find a feast of companionship, of peace, of clarity, and of wisdom.

As we grow more comfortable in our relationship with God, we can see that many of the same characteristics are desirable in our relationship with others. We can get a better grip on what our lives are about and how we fit into the grand scheme of things.

It's time to grab a new shopping cart and go looking for what really satisfies.

THREE

A Place
to Belong

hen my sister, Kim, and I were
teenagers, the Smith house was
always like Grand Central Station.
My mom said that she was never
sure who she would find sleeping on the living room
floor when she got up in the morning. That's
because all our friends loved hanging out there.
Mom, with her ultimate servant's heart, was always
making something good to eat for whoever happened to pass through.

She and Dad now admit they had a hidden
agenda. It was a great way to make sure they knew
where we were. If we were hanging out with friends
who wanted to be at our house, my folks rarely had
to worry about us.

Looking back on those days, I realize what an

incredible blessing it was to grow up in a home where love was abundant. Many people are still searching for what I sometimes took for granted. Even if your home is not warm and inviting, you can still find a place to belong.

What are the qualities that characterize such a place? Here are some considerations.

A Place Where People Give You Complete Acceptance

Karen Dean, a great Christian educator, often recites this sentence: "Nobody has lost the need for a place where, when you go there, they have to let you in and where, at the very least, you can wake without surprise."

I'm not sure any of us ever outgrows our need to be accepted. That's why the story of the prodigal son never loses its power. Even if you know it by heart, relive it with me.

The younger of two sons received his inheritance from his father and moved far away where he spent all he had on partying. When his money was gone, so were his so-called friends. To make matters worse, famine struck the land.

He was broke, and, with the times being tough on everyone, no one was eager to be generous. Finally, he got the undesirable job of feeding pigs, and his situation was so desperate he longed to fill his stomach with what they were eating. Humbled and hungry, he came to his senses and headed home, hoping that his father would take him in as a hired hand.

Get a mental picture of what happened next. "When he was still a great way off, his father saw him and had compassion, and ran and fell on his neck and kissed him" (Luke 15:20 NKJV). Instead of lecturing his wayward son about the mistakes he had made or giving the boy a probation period to prove himself, the father ran to greet him. Then, overcome with joy, he threw a celebration in honor of his son's return.

Just as the son whose father welcomed him home, we all desire a place where we are completely accepted.

I can think of nowhere that provides a better example of complete acceptance than at Nashville's Crisis Pregnancy Support Center. "People come here because we do everything in our power to make this a safe place," said Luci Freed. "We assure our clients that we will love them no matter what—whether they keep their babies, allow them to be adopted, or choose to go elsewhere and have an abortion. A lot of times we're the only ones willing to help a woman pick up the pieces after she's made wrong decisions." As testimony to their faithful ministry, since 1983 more than 14,000 women have been helped by the loving support and encouragement found at the center.

Their ministry is a beautiful portrait of what love and acceptance looks like, just as Paul described in 1 Corinthians 13:

> Love is kind and patient,
> never jealous, boastful, proud, or rude.
> Love isn't selfish or quick tempered.
> It doesn't keep a record of wrongs that
> others do.
> Love rejoices in the truth, but not in evil.
> Love is always supportive, loyal, hopeful,
> and trusting.
> Love never fails! (vv. 4–8 CEV)

Even if you are dealing with the finest, nicest people in the world, these standards are pretty hard to live up to. But here's the kicker. Look at the lives of the people who made up the church Paul was addressing. According to 1 Corinthians 6:9–10, they were formerly thieves, party animals, idolaters, and swindlers. In effect, God is urging us to accept people despite their background—and always help them move closer to His perfect love.

Even if you haven't found a place of true refuge yet, I believe someone will accept you completely if you hang in there with an open heart. It does exist! When you discover it, it will be a place where value is never taken for granted.

A Place Where People Recognize Your True Value

If I had to guess the number one problem teenagers face today, it would be lack of self-esteem. And, judging from the letters I receive, it's a struggle that doesn't magically disappear when you reach your twentieth birthday. If you ever question your worth, let me tell you, you're not alone.

Much of the problem stems from our world's messed-up viewpoint of personal value. The beautiful and the powerful people make the covers of magazines. And we're barraged by commercials that tell us we can buy what we need to make up for what we think we lack.

In stark contrast, look at the people Jesus valued. On numerous occasions He went out of His way to include those who seemed unlikely candidates to be embraced by the Son of God. His close circle of friends was an odd group of misfits—professional fishermen, a tax collector, and a political revolutionary. His followers included many who were considered the riffraff of society.

Even if you don't fit in anywhere else, know that Jesus sees you as a genuine treasure.

Melissa Trevathan, a Christian counselor for adolescents and my wife's youth minister when Deb was a teenager, told of seeing a note, scrawled in a child's handwriting, pinned to a bulletin board in a rural convenience store. It read: "Lost black cat. Answers to the name of Tom. He's ugly but I love him."

Melissa speculated that we can probably all identify with that cat at times. We feel lost and ugly, but it makes all the difference in the world to know that we are loved. The God of the entire universe says so. His Word testifies of it, and the cross is His irrefutable proof.

You probably know the verse that states so simply: "For God so loved the world that He gave His only begotten Son, that whoever believes in Him should not perish but have everlasting life" (John 3:16 NKJV). If God loves us that much, there's no question that we have value.

Even society's outsiders don't escape Jesus' attention. We know that He talked Zacchaeus the tax collector out of a sycamore tree, Jesus stood His ground when a terrifying demon-possessed man came running His way from a graveyard, and He felt right at home with the people that so-called "decent folks" would keep at arm's length. People like Jenny.

Abused as a young girl, Jenny numbed the pain by seeking the attention of one guy after another. At age fourteen, she became pregnant and had an abortion. When she became pregnant again at sixteen, her sister encouraged her to leave the multitude of bad influences she faced in her small hometown. She urged Jenny to seek help at a place of refuge: the Crisis Pregnancy Support Center in Nashville, a place where she could find the complete acceptance we talked about earlier.

The staff helped Jenny find a Christian family to live with while she carried her baby to term and connected her with a youth group that extended God's grace to her.

One winter day she was visiting her obstetrician, a Christian who donated his services to the center. As she prepared to leave, he took her coat from the hook on the exam room door and opened it so she could slip her arms into the sleeves. All the way home, she talked about how he had treated her like a lady. No man had ever recognized Jenny as a person of value—only as a way to fulfill his sexual desires.

To the doctor, it was such a common courtesy, he didn't even remember his actions. To Jenny, however, it was a revelation. His gesture was a gift, a gentlemanly act from a person who expected nothing in return. For the first time in years, she began to think of herself as a person worthy of being loved and respected.

Jenny found a place where people gave her complete acceptance, a place where people recognized her true value—and a place where people were ready to extend a helping hand, the next quality that characterizes a place of refuge.

A Place Where People Are Ready to Help You

When it comes to living out our faith, the Bible provides plenty of evidence that actions speak louder than words. First John 3:18 pulls no punches: "My little children, let us not love in word or in tongue, but in deed and in truth" (NKJV).

That's the idea behind "Give It Away," a song that Wayne, Amy, and I wrote for the *Change Your World* album:

You can entertain compassion
For a world in need of care
But the road of good intentions

Doesn't lead to anywhere
'Cause love isn't love
Till you give it away
You gotta give it away[1]

The mark of someone who truly exemplifies Christ is their willingness to get in the trenches with you.

Let's say that you're trying to push a stalled car into a driveway. Which would you rather have: a person who reads you the owner's manual along with physics books that explain how much energy must be exerted to get that car where it belongs, or someone who offers a shoulder to help you push? It doesn't matter how much a person knows in this case; everything depends upon how much he or she is willing to get involved.

Although you probably think of the comedian Roseanne as a pretty tough woman, she once told an interviewer about her start in small, rowdy, comedy clubs where the crowds could be brutal. She said that her sister would go with her and stay at the rear of the room.

If Roseanne was heckled by an obnoxious

patron, her sister moved so that she was directly in the comedian's line of sight behind that member of the audience. Roseanne said that when she looked in that direction she didn't see the face of a cruel stranger; she saw the face of her loving sister.

Is there a place where you consistently turn for help? Maybe it's the person who has let you know that it's okay to call anytime—day or night. Or the youth pastor who has demonstrated again and again his or her love for you. Or the friend who'll always pick you up when you need a ride. Or the confidante who'll help you shoulder the load you're carrying.

Just as love keeps no record of your wrongs, true helpers keep no record of their "rights." They don't remind you of how many times they've helped you out of a jam, prayed for you, offered advice, or just listened to what was on your mind. Their giving is more than kindness; it's a way of life.

A place of true refuge is

- a place where people give you complete acceptance,
- a place where people recognize your true value,

- a place where people are ready to help you,
- and, finally, a place where people dare to draw close to you.

A PLACE WHERE PEOPLE
DARE TO DRAW CLOSE

Every year Kamp Kanakuk in Bransford, Missouri—through its I'm Third Foundation—hosts a series of special events for inner-city youth called Kids Across America. The kids who attend come from some of the most dangerous urban areas in the country, neighborhoods where hope is hard to find.

Rodney attended camp in the summer of 1997. In late-night conversations, his counselor pieced together the tragic life of this thirteen year old. His father left the family early. His mother was dying of AIDS. He scrounged in garbage cans for food.

With no genuinely supportive family or friends, he was easily recruited by a gang. He participated in crime and watched violence erupt all around him. One of his best friends was killed in a gang-related shooting a month before coming to camp.

Every day at Kanakuk, a loving staff, who demonstrated Christ's love by their attitudes and actions, surrounded Rodney. He participated in recreational activities and listened attentively as counselors presented gospel messages.

After just three days, he told his counselor: "This place is paradise. I don't ever want to leave."

On the day of his departure, Rodney's counselor looked frantically through the crowd of three hundred kids boarding buses. After looking all over the grounds, he finally spotted the boy walking toward him slowly.

Rodney handed him a pair of green shoelaces. "Will you take these and throw them away for me?"

The counselor looked puzzled, so Rodney explained, "This is gang stuff. I had it here at camp. Don't need it no more."

"Why's that?" the counselor asked.

"I've been thinking. I realize this place is paradise but really just 'cause of one reason—Jesus. I wanted to be taking paradise with me, so I asked Him in my life forever. Don't need the stuff no more. Got a new family, and you're part of it."

At last, Rodney found a place where people were willing to draw close and extend a hand of hope instead of a fist of anger. Instead of gaining respect by lowering his morals to go along with the gang, he found the One who could raise his vision to see that life was more than what he had always known.

Many of the stories recorded in the Gospels demonstrate how Jesus dared to draw close to those outside the faith. Lepers, for example, were not allowed to associate with healthy people. In fact, they were required by law to stay at least six feet away from others. They often lived on the outskirts of town and sometimes in the desolate regions.

Matthew 8 tells the story of a leper who worked his way through a crowd to get to Jesus. Such a reckless act easily could have resulted in severe punishment. This was obviously a desperate man willing to risk everything to be healed.

Get inside this man's head for a minute and feel what he must have felt. Everyone looked upon him in horror. Wherever he went, people shooed him away. He was required to yell, "Unclean! Unclean!" whenever he approached people as a warning for them to stay clear of him. Who knows how long it had been since he was treated like a normal person?

This outcast pleaded, "Lord, if You are willing, You can make me clean"(v. 2 NKJV).

Christ's response was radical. He reached out his hand and touched the man. Under Levitical law, that would have made Jesus ceremonially unclean himself, requiring a quarantine of several days. But suddenly there was no leper—only a grateful man who told everyone what Jesus had done for him.

What 1 Peter 2:9–10 says about us is absolutely true:

> You are God's chosen and special people.
> You are a group of royal priests and a
> holy nation. God has brought you out of
> darkness into his marvelous light. Now
> you must tell all the wonderful things that
> he has done. The Scriptures say,
> > "Once you were nobody. Now you
> > are God's people.
> > At one time no one had pity on you.
> > Now God has treated you with
> > kindness." (CEV)

We belong to God and to each other. But we shouldn't stop with that wonderful realization. We were meant to grow.

A PLACE TO GROW

 hen I was a sophomore, Ceredo-Kenova High School formed its first tennis team, and even though I had been playing only a few years, I was given the dubious honor of representing the school. I found myself facing guys who had been on the courts for years. Most were older, stronger, faster, and far more experienced. My win-loss record for the season was an embarrassing 1 and 15. (I'd have been completely wiped out if one guy hadn't been a no-show, giving me a win by default.)

Even though I was trounced in match after match, I improved tremendously by playing people better than I was. When the next season rolled around, I actually won a number of matches, and much of the credit is due to surviving the drubbing I took my first year.

Growing is rarely easy—but it's always good for us.

Growing Is Essential

Several of my friends have adopted babies from China or Eastern Europe. Because many of these precious little ones were kept in overcrowded orphanages, they lacked the individual care and affection that most parents give. It's quite common for these babies to be developmentally slow. Often they're shorter than normal. Doctors have a name for this phenomenon: failure to thrive.

What's absolutely awesome is that most of these babies and young children can actually catch up when reared by loving parents. Over time, they can gain weight, height, and skills they lack.

Right now your neighborhood, school, workplace, and even your church, is probably populated with at least a few people who are failing to thrive spiritually or emotionally. Maybe it's you I'm talking about.

Debbie and I had five kids in eight years so the idea of growing is something we know a lot about. I can't imagine what it would be like if they didn't mature. Now that all are school-aged, they can do a lot for themselves (which is a huge relief for Deb and me).

But what if they never moved forward? I'm in pretty good shape but I don't think I'd like the idea of carrying five children everywhere or changing diapers for all of them multiple times every day. And we don't have to, because they've moved on to new milestones in life just as adults can grow to new levels of maturity.

I know a couple who conducted a faith-driven experiment some years ago. They invited all the difficult people from their church to a cookout. Some had significant emotional problems; a few were capable of practically sucking the life out of others through the way they related. Still others were constantly complaining or had poor social skills. All were in the habit of gravitating toward people who seemed more emotionally healthy—and then quickly wearing out their welcome.

The husband said that an interesting metamorphosis took place when their guests assembled. At first, they milled around uncomfortably, looking for someone they could lean on. Perhaps unconsciously they realized that there was no one there to fill that void. Can you guess what happened?

They began initiating conversations, asking questions of each other, volunteering to help with preparation of the meal. They had become so comfortable leaning on others, they failed to grow as they should have. The hosts were thrilled to see how these people faced a sink or swim situation. They grew!

"God loves us the way we are," author and evangelist Leighton Ford said, "but He loves us too much to leave us that way." And I would contend that He loves us too much to leave, period.

It's amazing how many people have responded to "I'm Waiting for You," the closing song on *I'll Lead You Home*. It's a simple message that reminds us that Christ has not left us alone; He will return for us. In a way, it's a musical version of Philippians 1:6: "Being confident of this very thing, that He who has begun a good work in you will complete it until the day of Jesus Christ" (NKJV).

Responses to the song have blown me away. Several people have sent letters saying they accepted Jesus as their Lord and Savior when I was performing it. Others have said that it seemed like it was written just for them, a love note of encouragement directly from God. (I just got to deliver it!) The point is that even if your friends and family fail you—it's bound to happen sometime—God will always see you through.

Growing is essential—and God, who created everything in nature, knows a lot about growth.

Yet we often resist growth. Why? Because growing isn't easy. Just ask a girl named Lori.

GROWING ISN'T EASY

For years, Lori suffered from an intense lack of self-worth. She felt invisible when she walked down the halls of her school. She often cried herself to sleep, questioning why she had no real friends and why her life was so hard. Rarely would she express an opinion. Every day was met with an increasing timidity to face the world.

Eventually she came to see our friend, Melissa Trevathan. In counseling sessions, Melissa learned a great deal about Lori's life and concluded that the best way for this fifteen-year-old girl to begin to change was by having her meet regularly with Sandy, a girl who was a year older. At first, Lori was completely intimidated by this older friend. It seemed that Sandy was everything she wasn't—popular, athletic, outgoing, a strong Christian.

The two girls got together once or twice a week to hang out. In time, Lori began to realize that Sandy was not treating her as some sort of charity case but as a true friend. Whenever Sandy saw Lori slipping back into her shell, the older girl would quietly but firmly tell her: "Be a person." Certainly, there were some rough spots and setbacks in their relationship, but a year later Lori had transformed into a much stronger person. In fact, Lori began to mentor other girls whose problems she completely understood.

The hike up the mountain may seem like pure drudgery but the view from the top makes it all worthwhile. Just as Lori discovered, we may not enjoy "growing pains" but we can't be truly alive without them.

If you compared your life to a tree, how would you say you were faring? Are you withering or growing? Are you drying up or is your life producing fruit? Are your roots reaching down to provide what you need to prosper spiritually and emotionally?

Growing isn't easy, because there are many enemies of growth. Let's do a little Bible study in gardening.

Enemies of Growth

If you've spent much time in church, chances are good that you've heard a preacher tell about the four soils described by Jesus in Matthew 13:3b–8:

> Behold, a sower went out to sow. And as he sowed, some seed fell by the wayside; and the birds came and devoured them. Some fell on stony places, where they did not have much earth; and they immediately sprang up because they had no depth of earth. But when the sun was up they were scorched, and because they had no root they withered away. And some fell among thorns, and the thorns sprang up and choked them. But others fell on good ground and yielded a crop: some a hundredfold, some sixty, some thirty. (NKJV)

You must be on guard against the things that would thwart your growth as a believer. It's easy for distractions to pull our attention from what we really need to do. Just like the birds in the parable, lots of distractions are flapping around these days. Maybe TV is getting in the way of time that you know you need to be praying. Maybe you're hindered by fruitless arguments about spiritual trivia. Maybe a relationship with another person is leading you away from God.

There's a cost to ensure that your own spiritual soil is sufficient for your growth. You must invest time and attention to see any benefits. You also have to invite the Holy Spirit to soften your hard spots and to water your dry places.

Everyone deals with thorns in their lives—a busy schedule, wrong desires, bitterness, jealousy, materialism. Who knows how many different kinds of thorns there are? But they all share a common trait: they choke your spiritual health like a fist squeezing a sponge. It's much easier to weed them out when you first notice them instead of facing a major battle once they root deeply.

Growing isn't easy, but it's always worthwhile because growth helps us reach our potential.

Limitless Potential

You are in the process of becoming—that's the message of the song "Emily."

> *Caught in an endless time*
> *Waiting for a sign*
> *To show you where to go*
> *Lost in a silent stare*
> *Looking anywhere for answers you*
> *   don't know*
>
> *On a wire*
> *Balancing your dreams*
> *Hoping ends will meet their means*
> *But you feel alone*
> *Uninspired*
> *Well, does it help you to*
> *Know that I believe in you*
> *You're an angel waiting for wings—Emily* [1]

I'm going to let you in on a secret. "Emily" was really written for a guy. Wayne Kirkpatrick, the oldest of three brothers, wrote the lyrics with his youngest brother, Brent, in mind.

At the time, Wayne was just beginning to see incredible success as a songwriter and producer. The middle Kirkpatrick brother, Karey, had moved to Los Angeles where he was making great inroads into the film business. He has since received credit as a screenwriter for such well-known movies as *The Rescuers Down Under* and *James and the Giant Peach*.

Brent was still in high school with all the big questions like "What will you do with your life?" looming before him. Wayne wanted him to know that he was going to come into his own in God's timing.

Since the song was released back in 1986, I've heard from lots of Emilies and others who said the lyrics perfectly described what they were going through. The point is that you're going *through* it. This is just one leg of the marathon. Whatever you're facing, it will probably pass in time. And pretty soon, with God's help, you'll go from "getting through" life to actually making a difference in it.

FIVE

A PLACE TO MAKE A DIFFERENCE

ot long ago, I was signing autographs in a Christian bookstore when someone pulled me aside and said, "There's someone here who'd like to meet you." I was led through the crowd to an eight-year-old girl who was blind. My heart goes out to kids of all ages and especially to those who live life with added challenges.

I bent down and introduced myself, hoping to brighten her day. I was totally unprepared for what happened next. She asked if she could pray for me. I'd have been nuts to turn down such a sweet request. But this girl didn't just say a prayer—she prayed!

She laid her delicate little hands on me and commenced to cover me, my music, my family, my travels, and my fans with blessings. She prayed for God to make me bolder in my faith and stronger in my witness. I was stunned—and really humbled. I told several people afterward that this little girl really knew God, and I was convinced beyond the shadow of a doubt that the Lord is going to use her in big ways for His kingdom.

You don't have to be an adult, or physically perfect, to serve the Lord in a mighty way. The Bible is filled with unexpected heroes of faith.

SMALL STONE, BIG IMPACT

Consider David, the shepherd boy. He came into the picture when the Israelite army was being intimidated and humiliated by the giant Goliath (1 Sam. 17). He stood nine feet, nine inches tall. When David, then only a youth, heard Goliath's taunts, he was indignant and asked to battle the giant one-on-one.

"You are not able to go against this Philistine to fight with him; for you are a youth," King Saul replied, "and he a man of war from his youth" (v. 33 NKJV).

Not exactly a vote of confidence.

Nevertheless, Saul eventually allowed David to take the battlefield (the king had no other volunteers, believe me), much to Goliath's surprise. The giant warrior expected instant victory but the shepherd boy's words to him were prophetic: "You come to me with a sword, with a spear, and with a javelin. But I come to you in the name of the LORD of hosts, the God of the armies of Israel, whom you have defied. This day the LORD will deliver you into my hand, and I will strike you and take your head from you" (vv. 45–46 NKJV). Pretty tough talk from a kid who wasn't big enough to stand up in armor.

But did he have an impact? And how! He placed a stone in his sling and drove it right into Goliath's skull. When the Philistine army saw their hero hit the ground, they fled with the Israelite army in hot pursuit.

Who says you have to wait until you're old and wise to make a difference? Who says your body has to be whole for you to be wholly given over to God's purposes?

GIFTS AND WOUNDS

Christian communicator Landon Saunders believes that each person is a unique combination of gifts and wounds. The challenge, he says, is for the gifts to overcome the wounds before the wounds overcome the gifts. Paddling against the current is hard work but it's required if you want to get to your destination.

The essence of making a difference is making an effort.

When my friend Mike was in junior high, he met an older woman named Trudy. This lady absolutely oozed enthusiasm and encouragement. To an insecure guy like Mike, she was a gift from heaven. He'd say that he was thinking of trying out for a play at school. She would respond with cyclone force excitement, "Oh, you must! You'd be great!"

When he talked about his ambitions for school, she was 100 percent behind him. She'd say, "Oh, that's great! You're going to be at the top of your class."

When he graduated from college and started to work, she'd ask, "What wonderful thing are you involved in now?"

Her presence was so powerful, she could literally pull him out of a funk in just a few minutes of conversation. She was aware of his wounds but she was determined to help him focus on his gifts.

Years passed before they crossed paths at a party. Tearfully, he told her how much he appreciated her consistent encouragement during his trying teenage years. This time it was Trudy who was encouraged. "Aren't you sweet?" she said, wiping tears herself. "Mike, I'm an old woman and sometimes I wonder if my life has really mattered much. Hearing your kind words makes me believe that maybe it has." While others at the party looked on baffled, the two embraced as only dear friends can.

Trudy wasn't Mother Teresa or Anne Frank or Corrie ten Boom. Her life story will never be made into a movie but she is one of the countless millions who are simply faithful to use what God has given her.

USING YOUR TALENTS

Perhaps you know the story of the wealthy man

who called three of his servants and placed his finances in their keeping:

> And to one he gave five talents [the
> equivalent of 30,000 days' wages for
> an average laborer], to another two,
> and to another one, to each according
> to his own ability; and immediately he
> went on a journey. Then he who had
> received the five talents went and traded
> with them, and made another five talents.
> And likewise he who had received two
> gained two more also. But he who had
> received one went and dug in the ground,
> and hid his lord's money. After a long
> time the lord of those servants came
> and settled accounts with them"
> (Matt. 25:15–19 NKJV).

The man was very pleased with the servants who doubled his money but harshly demanded that the third servant defend his actions. His response was tragic: "I was afraid, and went and hid your talent in the ground. Look, there you have what is yours" (v. 25 NKJV). For his foolish actions, this servant was severely punished.

How tragic to bury your talents instead of using them for God's glory! Someone is probably thinking, *But I don't really have any talents to make a difference in anyone's life.*

Please hear me out. If you can make a child laugh, mow a lawn, cook a meal, drive a car, sing a song, wash dishes, talk on the phone, read a book, or say a prayer, you can make a difference in someone's life.

Every year *USA Weekend*, the Sunday magazine supplement in many newspapers, sponsors its "Make A Difference" contest, encouraging people all across the country to do something to affect the lives of those around them or the environment in which we live. It's amazing how creative people get.

Through this one event, all kinds of wonderful things happen. Houses get repaired. Homeless people get warm, new socks. Community centers get painted. Trash-strewn neighborhoods get cleaned up. Food gets distributed to people in need. And those are just a few of the efforts.

You don't have to wait for a special event to do something special for others. Ever heard this statement: "Somebody ought to do something"? What they really mean is somebody else ought to do something. Perhaps people who say this ought to examine their own hearts to see if the call is going out to them. Maybe that is God's way of calling your name.

What you do doesn't have to be impressive. Jesus said, "Anyone who gives one of my most humble followers a cup of cool water, just because that person is my follower, will surely be rewarded" (Matt. 10:42 cev). Just a cup of water. Who couldn't do that?

THE HUMILITY OF GIVING

While on the Amy Grant Christmas Tour in 1997, I had the opportunity to experience both the joy and humility of what it means to help. Wess Stafford, president of Compassion International, pulled me aside about an hour before the doors opened at Charlotte Coliseum in North Carolina and asked me to go with him.

We walked out onto the stage, and he told me to look around. I wasn't sure what he had in mind.

The place was empty except for crew members making last-minute preparations for the concert.

"I want you to imagine that every seat you see here is filled with a child sponsored through Compassion International," Wes said, "because that's how many kids have been sponsored by people who've signed up after one of your concerts or filled out one of the forms that are inserted in your albums."

To think about how many kids were being given a chance to break out of poverty and were being taught about Jesus because my fans were moved to make a difference was totally humbling. If you know how emotional I am when it comes to kids, I don't have to tell you I was totally speechless. It didn't take long for tears to well up in my eyes.

We all know how good it is to receive but the words of Acts 20:35 are absolutely true: "Remember the words of the Lord Jesus, that He said, 'It is more blessed to give than to receive'" (NKJV).

You were made to be still and know that He is God but also to realize that "in Him we live and move and have our being" (Acts 17:28 NKJV). It's when we move out under His guidance that we get a sense of joy.

In the great movie *Chariots of Fire*, Scottish missionary and Olympic runner Eric Liddell spoke of his passion for serving God as well as the thrill he got from his sport. "When I run, I feel His pleasure," he said with great conviction.

As we step out to make a difference in our world, we feel God's pleasure as He stirs within us. Now we just need to look for the place to begin.

SIX

A Place to Start

o you know the first question found in the Bible? It was posed by God to Adam and Eve when they tried to hide from Him: "Where are you?"

God's question to them is worthy of your consideration. Where are you? The right answer is not your bedroom, your dorm, or sitting under a tree. Take a moment to consider seriously how you would answer the following questions. You might even want to write down your responses.

Where Are You Spiritually?

I don't know that I've ever heard anyone say they are far more spiritually mature than they expected. We always want to be a little further down the road. None of us have arrived. Most of us are straining just to move forward.

Where does this day find you? Are you on fire

for God, or spiritually numb? Is your heart wide open to His possibilities? Consider these questions for a little self-evaluation:

- When was the last time you gained new insight from reading God's Word?
- Do you pray with the firm belief that God is listening?
- Do you look forward to worshiping God?
- When was the last time you expressed sincere gratitude to God?
- Do you find your best intentions being neutralized by sin?
- Are you willing to forgive others?
- Do you feel a sense of compassion for those around you who are hurting?
- How long has it been since you've experienced a true sense of joy?

We're not giving scores, but your answers to these questions should give you some idea on where you are spiritually.

Where Are You Emotionally?

"Life just isn't as much fun as a McDonald's commercial." Those words of wisdom were offered by a media savvy junior high student. She's right. Every day is not blue skies and rainbows. Some days we dance on mountaintops; other days find us dragging through dark valleys.

We sometimes don't quite know the proper place for our emotions. Some people are controlled by them, carried away by spiritual highs and devastated by the low points of life's harsh realities. Others treat their emotions as enemies sent to undermine their firm control of an orderly life; they aren't comfortable with feelings and don't like the idea of anyone else letting their humanity show.

Obviously the answer is somewhere between these two extremes.

A great promise from Christ fits in perfectly here: "If the Son makes you free, you shall be free indeed" (John 8:36 NKJV). I think there are two kinds of freedom as it relates to emotions: freedom *from* and freedom *to.*

I don't have to convince you of the negative effects of being ruled by compulsive behavior, guilt, shame, anger, fear, anxiety, or regret. Jesus came to give us freedom from things that enslave us. Some people find themselves miraculously set free in an instant. Most, however, find that it takes months and years of changing thought patterns and breaking old habits.

As we realize that we are no longer prisoners of sin and shame, Christ gives us freedom to love without strings attached. We can be relentless in our love, letting God's compassion flow through us and on to others.

To explore where you are emotionally, respond to the following questions:

- Is your general outlook on life hopeful?
- Do you use anger to keep people at a distance?
- When was the last time you had a good laugh?
- Are you moved with compassion when you see others in pain?
- Do you handle conflict appropriately?
- Do the hard times of the past rob you of your ability to enjoy the good things today?
- Are you aware of what others are feeling?

- Are you ashamed to show emotions?
- Are you approachable?
- Do you allow boredom to control you?
- Can you learn from your mistakes and move on with a good attitude?

If you need help to gain a perspective on your emotional health, try two things. First, ask a trusted friend to talk through these questions with you and offer objective insights. Remember that you want honesty—not comments that are too kind or too critical.

Second, test yourself using Matthew 12:34 as your guide: "Out of the abundance of the heart the mouth speaks" (NKJV). Notice the character of what you say. Are your conversations peppered with sarcasm, fear, or uncertainty? Or are they seasoned with grace, understanding, and hopefulness? What you hear yourself saying will tell you where to focus your attention and where change is needed. It will also reveal your progress—don't forget to thank God for moving you forward!

Where Are You Financially?

I won't go into the gory details, but I will admit that Debbie and I got into a financial mess when we were first married and money was tight. Our credit card spending was out of control, and we didn't have the cash to pay the bills. Not smart.

Over the years, we've wised up and become more responsible, but I know how getting things out of whack financially can really mess with your peace of mind. It can also put you at odds with God's plan for using the resources He has given you.

If you're living at home and all your needs are provided for, you may not need to think too much about money. If, however, you're making most or all of your financial decisions, it's important to give it some thought. Researchers say that the majority of Americans are in tremendous debt, running up massive charges on their credit cards that they'll spend years paying off.

Even if you're fairly carefree, you probably spend some time thinking about finances. If you're wondering how you're going to make the payments on your car, your automobile insurance, or your credit card bill, it's undoubtedly influencing all aspects of your life.

I'm no financial consultant but this much I know: God doesn't want you to be preoccupied with money—not with making huge sums of it or living in fear because you haven't controlled the spending of what you have.

If you're in a bad place with your finances, seek out people who will guide you toward peace of mind through wise spending. If you're making smart decisions with money, keep on that path. It'll save you a lot of worry and make you a better steward of what God has given you.

Where Are You Mentally?

Some who are reading this page are brilliant. You'll speed-read your way through this book and half of a dictionary before bedtime. Others, like me, breathed a sigh of relief when they received their high school diploma. Although major mental power may make a huge difference on college entrance exams or employment tests, God grades our lives on His own gracious curve. His guideline was simple and straightforward—to love Him with all your heart and with all your soul and with all your mind (Matt. 22:37).

The mental capacity of a Harvard honor student far surpasses what a musician like me has to offer. But God asks us both the same question: are you loving Me with all you have?

When it comes to the practical side of life, Paul added this admonishment, "Whatever you do, do it heartily, as to the Lord and not to men" (Col. 3:23 NKJV).

Are you applying yourself mentally to the tasks before you? Are you working at your school assignments or job tasks with all your heart, realizing that God notices your effort and is glorified when you give your best? Are you reaching your potential by exercising your brain, or becoming a mental couch potato?

If you're not learning something new, you're leaning on the past.

Where Are You Physically?

You don't have to be picture perfect physically. Actually that's a goal hardly worth striving for. If all you're doing is working to impress people when you walk by, you're reinforcing the lie that it's the external part of a person that matters most. In contrast, check out God's perspective: "For the LORD does not see as man sees; for man looks at the outward appearance, but the LORD looks at the heart" (1 Sam. 16:7b NKJV).

So is the physical aspect of our lives completely unimportant? No, there's more to the story. Consider what 1 Corinthians 6:19–20 says about treating your body with respect: "Do you not know that your body is the temple of the Holy Spirit who is in you, whom you have from God, and you are not your own? For you were bought at a price; therefore glorify God in your body and in your spirit, which are God's" (NKJV).

The Lord won't direct you to devote your life to looking like a supermodel. He's simply telling us to do our best to take care of what He's given us.

TAKING OTHERS TO WHERE YOU WANT TO BE

So far, I've focused on the places you're looking for. Now let me turn that around to say that it's your job to help others find a place of acceptance, a place to grow, and a place to make a difference. Remember how Lori was really helped by her friend Sandy? It's your responsibility to be a Sandy to others.

Our society seems to think our highest calling is to self-fulfillment. It's the old "he who dies with the most toys wins" mentality. Let me set the record straight. He who dies with the most toys still dies. The greater goal is to leave a legacy so that the seeds we plant continue to grow long after we're gone— seeds of hope, of encouragement, of challenge, of faith. Remember that "everybody has a seed to sow."

This is merely doing what God calls us to do, an act of simple obedience and reverence. It is not somehow elevating ourselves by doing good works. Rich Mullins once said something like this: "Christ died for sinners. We're all hung up with trying to impress God with how good we are, and He is not impressed."

There's an interesting twist in the story that Jesus tells to describe the day of judgment:

> The righteous will answer Him, saying,
> "Lord when did we see You hungry and
> feed You, or thirsty, and give You drink?
> And when did we see You a stranger,
> and invite You in, or naked and clothe
> You? And when did we see You sick, or
> in prison, and come to You?" And the

King will answer and say to them,
"Truly, I say to you, to the extent that
you did it to one of these brothers of
Mine, even the least of them, you did it
to Me." (Matt. 25:37–40 NASB)

The righteous just went along, caring about
people, meeting their needs without making a big
deal out of it. In fact, they needed the King (God) to
remind them of when they did such things. Yet, their
concern for others earned them God's highest praise.
They were obedient servants attending to their master's business.

That applies to much more than the narrow
view of "God's work." Your testimony should be
seen in whatever you do. If you work at a store in
the mall, show great attention and kindness to
everyone who walks in the door. If you wait tables
in a restaurant, treat your customers as you would
Christ Himself. If you baby-sit, love those kids the
way Jesus would. If you're an employer, let your
workers see the grace and wisdom of God in your
actions. Be a refuge for people who walk down the
halls of your school.

Using Paul's simple summation: "Whether you eat or drink, or whatever you do, do all to the glory of God" (1 Cor. 10:31 NKJV).

Now that we have a "place" to call home, let's consider what we're doing here—our purpose.

PART 2

PURPOSE

Where we're going
with our lives, our mission,
the reason we're here

SEVEN

THE PURPOSE
OF PURPOSE

hen I started Rocketown Records in
1996, I wanted to create a small,
personal label that nurtured new talent, just as Michael Blanton and
Dan Harrell had done when they started Reunion
Records in 1982 to give Kathy Troccoli and me a
launching pad. I wasn't interested in being trendy—
I wanted to establish a home for artists I believed
had something important to say and provide a men-
toring role for people who created Christian music.

Because I'm definitely not the right person to
run the day-to-day operations of a record label, my
friend Don Donahue who formerly worked for
Reunion came on board as president. We spent hours
talking about the exciting possibilities before us and
agreed that our trademark should be great songs.

When people heard that we were starting a label, we were flooded with tapes and phone calls. Some aspiring artists were genuinely humble. Some were, uh, not. Those in the latter category quickly fell out of consideration because we weren't looking for people whose goal was to "be a star."

As we were exploring our options for a debut album, Don remembered songs by a singer/songwriter named Chris Rice whom he had heard while working at Reunion. Three of them were ultimately recorded by Kathy Troccoli on her *Sounds of Heaven* album—"Hallelujahs," "Missing You," and "Go Light Your World."

Don gave me a custom CD that Chris had made with Nashville producer Monroe Jones. I was blown away by his talent as a writer, vocalist, and guitarist. In fact, I was moved to tears listening to "Welcome to Our World," a song I recorded for my second Christmas album *Christmastime*.

Chris seemed like just the kind of artist we wanted, so we scheduled a meeting to talk to him. From the moment he walked in the door, we knew we were dealing with someone with humble confidence. Instead of dressing to impress us, he arrived in cut-off jeans and a T-shirt from a camp where he had just been the featured musician.

"You guys need to know something up front," Chris told us. "Doing camps and retreats with teenagers—that's the reason I'm alive. If I could never sing again, I would still do what I do."

We talked for a long time about his experiences in ministering to students, and our conversation ended with Chris's gentle directness. "I'd be glad to do a record with you, but I won't let you try to change who I am or what I do."

After he left, Don and I were more enthusiastic about him than ever. Here was a guy who was completely unimpressed by the possibility of becoming well-known as an artist. Instead, he was so focused on his ministry, he had no time to be distracted by other things.

As you probably know, Chris was the first artist to record for Rocketown Records. His album, *Deep Enough to Dream*, surprised many music executives by selling over 150,000 copies with none of the hype that sometimes accompanies new releases. He was even nominated for six Dove Awards including New Artist of the Year in 1998.

Although I respect Chris as a musician, I admire him much more for the way he identified his purpose in life and holds fast to it.

Many people these days don't seem to have the clear sense of purpose that Chris does. They're like boats without rudders. They drift from place to place, relationship to relationship. They not only do not chart a course, they don't even stay anchored anywhere.

THE WHATEVER GENERATION

The next time you're talking with a group of your friends, listen for a one-word response that characterizes our times: *whatever*.

"Do you want to go to the mall?"

"Whatever."

"I don't think it's a big deal to have sex before marriage."

"Whatever."

"Don't you believe in God?"

"Whatever."

Some people have started to refer to youth culture as the Whatever Generation.

Sociologists say that "whatever" characterizes our lack of conviction and purpose. It's not that we're so flexible—it's that we're so ungrounded. We constantly shift because nothing much matters.

Some years ago, a teenage boy hung himself from the only tree of any size in a trendy new neighborhood. Upwardly mobile families had recently relocated there by the thousands. His suicide note said, "This tree is the only thing around here with any roots."

You can see that rootlessness turn outward in anger with increasing frequency. I've been sickened and saddened by the growing number of senseless violent acts by teenagers in America—drive-by shootings, assaults on teachers, school massacres. As I watch these stories on the news, I'm struck with how numb the perpetrators seem to be. They stand before judges emotionless. As the charges against them are read, you can almost imagine them shrugging their shoulders and saying, "Whatever."

Of course, there are plenty of other destructive possibilities available that are less sensational than these violent acts. You can devote yourself to being the life of the party. You can keep a private stash of the temptation that drives away the hurt in your life—alcohol, drugs, pornography. The world offers many inadequate ways to cope with what troubles you. But do any of these actually move your life forward? Of course not. They're merely diversions and distractions.

Where is the strong sense of purpose that serves as a rudder for our lives? Fortunately the Bible is rich with examples that can give us direction.

SETTING FORTH

Let's start with the Greek root word for purpose: *prothesis*. It means to set something forth, placing it in plain view, laying it out for all to see.

Imagine you're the captain of a ship one hundred years ago. You pull out a map to chart your course from your current port to your new destination. You must consider the tides, the winds, your sails, your cargo, and the seaworthiness of your ship. Once you have calculated how these will affect your progress, you set sail. You know where you're going, and you have some useful guides to help you get there.

That's a good mental picture of what it means to have purpose. You find the word *prothesis* in verses like Romans 8:28, which says, "We know that all things work together for good to those who love God, to those who are the called according to His purpose" (NKJV). In Eugene Peterson's paraphrase of the New Testament, called *The Message*, he expresses the idea this way: "We can be so sure that every detail in our lives of love for God is worked into something good. God knew what He was doing from the very beginning." God knew what he was doing and did it. As obedient servants, His purpose becomes our purpose.

How confident are we that we know what we are doing? Are we guided by purpose?

The book of Esther in the Old Testament presents a great illustration of what it means to have purpose.

FOR SUCH A TIME AS THIS

Travel back to Persia, approximately 475 B.C. King Xerxes was auditioning many beautiful women to be his new bride. Esther, a young Jewish maiden, was among those brought to the palace, and, after all the candidates were considered, she was selected to be his queen.

Some time later, her uncle Mordecai asked for help in thwarting a plan to wipe out all Jews in the kingdom.

When Esther seemed resistant, Mordecai replied, "Do not think in your heart that you will escape in the king's palace any more than all the other Jews. For if you remain completely silent at this time, relief and deliverance will arise for the Jews from another place, but you and your father's house will perish. Yet who knows whether you have come to the kingdom for such a time as this?" (4:13–14 NKJV).

She summoned all her courage and convinced the king to withdraw his order. In every way, she lived up to her purpose.

Now, I have a question for you. Who knows whether *you* have come to live for such a time as this? Have you ever thought that you were born for a distinct reason? Could it be that you live to accomplish a unique purpose in God's kingdom?

Who, me? you're probably asking. *I'm not Esther. I'm not Mother Teresa. I'm not Billy Graham. There aren't even that many people who know who I am.* That may be true, but don't ever let your perspective overshadow the fact that you were born for a purpose, just like Angelita Ruis.

In the Mexican border town of Reynosa, Angelita, a woman well into her eighties, was healed of a heart problem. Although she stood less than five feet tall, Angelita Ruis was a giant of faith. As an expression of gratitude for what God had done for her, she prayed for an opportunity to serve. God opened the door for her to live and work in a nursing home for poor and neglected elderly people.

The facility was equipped with a good washing machine and dryer, so she decided to put them to use for God's purposes. She offered free laundry services to anyone in the community who needed clean clothes. When they came to her with a bag of laundry, she used the opportunity to tell them what God had done for her and how much He loved them. Over the years, a number of people accepted Christ while waiting for their clothes to be washed.

Angelita wasn't a queen. Her actions didn't dramatically save a whole nation of people. She just washed clothes and talked about Jesus. She knew her purpose and hit upon a unique way of living true to it.

Now, you may be thinking that there is some reason why you can't serve God as Esther and Angelita did. Don't let your excuses get in the way of what God might want to accomplish through you. Excuses didn't stop Moses hundreds of years ago.

"SEND SOMEONE ELSE"

If Moses had gone to see a therapist, he might have discovered that he struggled with severe self-esteem issues. When God called him to lead the people of Israel, he tried to wiggle out of the assignment: "But suppose they will not believe me or listen to my voice; suppose they say, 'The LORD has not appeared to you'" (Ex. 4:1 NKJV).

To answer this question God demonstrated His power and presence with several miraculous signs. Then was Moses ready to set out?

"I have never been a good speaker. I wasn't one before you spoke to me, and I'm not one now. I am slow at speaking, and I can never think of what to say," (4:10 CEV) Moses insisted.

You might think that God was ready to give this guy a swift kick in the pants, but instead the Lord affirmed who He is: "Who makes people able to speak or makes them deaf or unable to speak? Who gives them sight or makes them blind? Don't you know that I am the one who does these things? Now go! When you speak, I will be with you and give you the words to say" (4:11–12 CEV).

You can almost hear the hysteria in Moses' voice as he begged, "LORD, please send someone else to do it" (4:13 CEV). At that, God told him to take his brother Aaron to be his spokesman. "Get on with the program," He said, in effect.

And Moses did. We remember him as the man who led the Israelites out of captivity. Although there were a few stumbling episodes in his walk of faith, his life is summed up this way: "There has not arisen in Israel a prophet like Moses, whom the LORD knew face to face, in all the signs and wonders which the LORD sent him to do in the land of

Egypt, before Pharaoh, before all his servants, and in all his land, and by all that mighty power and all the great terror which Moses performed in the sight of all Israel" (Deut. 34:10–12 NKJV).

God had a purpose in mind when He chose Moses. And Moses overcame his wobbly start to become a mighty man of faith. So, if you feel like you've been bumbling around, take heart. You're not alone. In fact, you're in good company.

There's a line, said in mock-seriousness in the movie *Blues Brothers*, that can be taken literally by us as Christians: "We're on a mission from God." In the grand scheme of things, it is very clear what we're to be about. As we will see in the next chapter, our obvious ambition is spelled out in a number of ways in Scripture.

EIGHT

OUR NOT-SO-SECRET AMBITION

riginally there was just a melody and a title—"Secret Ambition." Wayne Kirkpatrick and I brainstormed what the song might be about. At one time, we were thinking it could be a tribute to Martin Luther King Jr. Eventually, we went with something a little more obvious. When Wayne and Amy Grant had finished the lyrics, it was a unique way to explore Christ's life.

Nobody knew His secret ambition
Nobody knew His claim to fame
He broke the old rules steeped in tradition
He tore the holy veil away

Questioning those in powerful position

Running to those who called His name
'Cause nobody knew His secret ambition
Was to give His life away [1]

Although Jesus confused and confounded the people around Him, we have the benefit of looking back through time to see how clearly He pursued His purpose. No one person or thing could keep Him from being about His Father's business.

When Satan tempted Him with food, pride, and power, He refused to give in. Instead, He responded to the enemy's schemes with Scripture (Matt. 4:1–11). After Jesus miraculously fed over five thousand people, a group of them prepared to use force to make Him king but He slipped away and headed for the mountain to be alone (John 6:15). When Jesus told His disciples that He would be betrayed, killed, and raised again, Peter blurted out, "This shall not happen to you!" Jesus' reply was a strong rebuke because He knew that was exactly why He came into the world (Matt. 16:21–23 NKJV).

Obviously we were not born to take on the sins of the world as Jesus did, but we are to use His life as our example. Just what does He ask of us?

One way to answer that question is to consider ourselves among His disciples when He made this simple statement: "Follow me." We go where He leads. We trace His steps. We do what He does.

After living with His disciples for three years, Jesus retreated with them to have a private time of fellowship and instruction. As a demonstration of the attitude they should have, He took a towel and basin of water and washed His disciples' dusty, weary feet. Because they were obviously baffled by His actions, He explained himself in John 13:

> "Do you understand what I have done?
> You call me your teacher and Lord, and
> you should, because that is who I am.
> And if your Lord and teacher has washed
> your feet, you should do the same for
> each other. I have set the example, and
> you should do for each other exactly
> what I have done for you. I tell you for
> certain that servants are not greater than
> their master, and messengers are not
> greater than the one who sent them.

You know these things, and God will bless you if you do them." (vv. 12b–17 CEV)

In the same conversation, He added this directive: "You must love each other, just as I have loved you. If you love each other, everyone will know that you are my disciples" (John 13:34–35 CEV).

Jesus is our ultimate role model. If we follow His example and do what He says, we'll stay out of trouble and on the path of becoming who we're meant to be. He has given us an intriguing promise that continues to blow my mind: "I tell you for certain that if you have faith in me, you will do the same things that I am doing. You will do even greater things, now that I am going back to the Father. Ask me, and I will do whatever you ask. This way the Son will bring honor to the Father. I will do whatever you ask me to do" (John 14:12–14 CEV).

Still, there are times when we wish that Christ would spell it out for us as clearly as he did for Paul on the Damacus road. A blinding light from heaven shone upon him, causing Paul to fall to the ground. Then a voice left nothing to speculation: "I am Jesus, whom you are persecuting. But rise and stand on your feet; for I have appeared to you for this purpose, to make you a minister and a witness both of the things which you have seen and of the things which I will yet reveal to you" (Acts 26:15–16 NKJV). Although you probably haven't had Jesus appear to you, the charge given to Paul is fitting for each of us as believers. Even if we aren't confronted by a blinding light and a voice from heaven, our calling and our purpose is quite clear.

MY UTMOST FOR HIS HIGHEST

One of my favorite daily devotional books is Oswald Chambers' *My Utmost for His Highest*. It begins with reflections on Paul's writings in the book of Philippians: "I honestly expect and hope that I will never do anything to be ashamed of. Whether I live or die, I always want to be as brave as I am now and bring honor to Christ" (1:20 CEV).

The devotional message includes these thoughts: "(Jesus) has asked us to yield to him. It's as if Paul were saying, 'My determined purpose is to be my utmost for His highest—my best for His glory'. . . Paul was determined that nothing would stop him from doing exactly what God wanted." [2]

To respond with such passion is more than simple obedience; it is an exciting revelation. You are entering into an eternal partnership with the Creator of everything, taking a vow of loyalty that can never be compromised or broken, making a lifelong pledge of service to His "love crusade."

ADVENTURES IN FAITH

I love adventure movies like *Braveheart* and the *Star Wars* series, almost anything that seems bigger than life. Not surprisingly, I'm a huge fan of the *Indiana Jones* movies. In fact, I used to have a giant poster from *Raiders of the Lost Ark* hanging in my studio. There was a lot I didn't like about the first sequel, *Indiana Jones and the Temple of Doom*, but one idea really struck me hard.

Near the end of the movie, Indiana escaped from his captors but refused to head for safety until he freed the children who were being forced to work in mines beneath the evil sultan's city. He said something like this: "We're not leaving here without the kids."

The movie came out about the time we were taking the *Go West, Young Man* tour on the road. Michael Blanton and I got really excited when we realized that we could say the same thing, although with a different meaning. Whereas Indiana Jones wanted to lead the children to the city they came from, our hearts were set on leading them to a real relationship with God.

It challenged us, encouraged us, and helped us "set forth" every night with a clear understanding that we weren't stepping on stage just to perform. We were there for a purpose—and that purpose was to draw people to God.

That can be done in a million ways. Angelita did it by washing clothes. Joe White does it by bringing kids to Kamp Kanakuk for some great times they'll never forget. Franklin Graham does it by preaching and delivering all kinds of aid to people in need through Samaritan's Purse, his non-profit evangelistic organization. If you ask him about his purpose, he'll tell you flatly, "The only thing you need to know about me is that I'm out to win souls for Christ."

How do you do it?

Keep It Simple

I get my purpose in life from a confrontation recorded in Matthew 22:36–39. A lawyer, hoping to trap Jesus, asked him, "Teacher, which is the great commandment in the law?" Jesus replied, " 'You shall love the LORD your God with all your heart, with all your soul, and with all your mind.' This is the first and great commandment. And the second is like it: 'You shall love your neighbor as yourself' " (NKJV).

If you think about it, you can obtain guidance in almost every possible situation if you let the Holy Spirit speak to you through these verses. They will help you work through relationships with friends, guide you in making ethical decisions, guard your morality, and keep you from places where you shouldn't be.

I love this statement from St. Francis of Assisi: "Preach the gospel to all the world. If necessary, use words." His approach is even simpler than mine. His thought, however, is revolutionary. Our greatest witness is through actions that are consistent with our words.

That's the foundational truth behind "Live the Life," a song that Brent Bourgeois and I wrote as the theme song for the Youth for Christ Conference DC / LA '97. The lyrics in the chorus spell the message out plainly:

For the world to know the truth
There can be no greater proof
Than to live the life
Live the life

There's no love that's quite as pure
There's no pain we can't endure
If we live the life
Live the life
Be a light for all to see
For every act of love will set you free [3]

THE GREATEST USE OF LIFE

Inside each Christian, a battle rages over yielding to God's call. The Holy Spirit encourages us to step out boldly in faith, to love people without fear of being hurt or rejected, to serve energetically and humbly, to worship with deep gratitude, and to draw people to salvation with real urgency.

Satan works on our emotions to keep us uncertain, frustrated, self-centered, fearful, or downhearted. He knows that if we don't comprehend God working in our own lives that we'll never get very far in reaching out to others.

"We want to save ourselves and keep ourselves and hold ourselves back as though the highest goal in life would be to look good in our caskets," wrote Reuben Welch in *We Really Do Need Each Other*. "It's no special blessing to come to the end of life with love unshared, selves ungiven, activities unactivated, deeds undone, emotions unextended." [4]

We were meant to seize the day, to make every moment count for God's kingdom. I like something psychologist William James said, "The great use of life is to spend it for something that will outlast it."

Fulfilling our purpose will last longer than a lifetime. In fact, it's eternal. Sometimes though, the roads we travel after we set forth are not the ones we anticipate.

U N E X P E C T E D
P A T H S

 ven though my wife, Debbie, is due truckloads of flowers for all she does, being a mom with a large family isn't what she thought her life would be like. When she was in college, she was confident that God had given her a heart for the poor so she worked out an educational plan that would lead her in that direction. She planned to get a master's degree in public health nursing, marry a doctor, and spend her life opening clinics in Appalachia or Haiti.

She finished college without finding that doctor to marry. After going on a short-term missions project to Haiti, which led her to have second thoughts about the direction she was pursuing, Debbie came back to Nashville. Soon after that, we met and our lives took turns that were far from what we expected. As you could probably guess, I have no plans to become a doctor, although it sure would come it handy when I have a house full of sick kids.

Instead of moving on to the mission field, Debbie's ministry has been to our kids—and what a great job she does! She also provides a much-needed reality check for me. At times when I've been attracted to the glitz of the music business, she's always been there to put things in perspective and remind me of the things that really matter.

Interestingly, God has opened doors for us to be connected to the poor in other ways. We've been involved with Compassion International for over ten years, sponsoring two kids who will soon be adults. The Lord has also given opportunities for us to help Samaritan's Purse, Habitat for Humanity, and other organizations that work with the poor in the United States and around the world.

Because our kids are getting older and don't need their mom as much as they once did, the Lord is opening new doors for Debbie to serve. Debbie has stumbled onto some unexpected paths.

SPEAKING IN THE SILENCE

A few years ago, Debbie suddenly lost her voice and was diagnosed with a problem that usually affects only elderly people. Immediately we called all our friends to pray for her healing.

Around that time, three people came to Debbie independently and told her that they believed God was going to use her to speak to women. The timing seemed bizarre, almost cruel. But in a short time, the vocal problem went away as mysteriously as it appeared.

Debbie has never thought of herself as a public speaker, but opportunities are coming her way with increasing frequency. And I'm excited because she has so much to offer. Deb can speak on the pain of being a child of divorce, her battle with anorexia as a teenager, the challenges of being the mother of five kids, and the patience of being married to a guy who can sometimes be a real space cadet. Because she's been able to visit a number of poverty-stricken areas, she can even relate her firsthand encounters with the poor.

Although it's nothing like the life Deb had pictured for herself, it is well within the life purpose of following Jesus. God is simply providing paths that are quite surprising.

Sometimes these unexpected paths are difficult, like Debbie's voice problem. At times like these we all tend to ask, "Why?"

THE BIG QUESTION: WHY?

"Why?" is one of the hardest questions to grapple with. Why did my friends lose their baby after only two days of life? Why does God allow people to endure years of suffering, as Christine probably has experienced, or abuse? Why do some single people spend a lifetime waiting for the right person to come along and never get to experience being married?

I don't have any answers that are going to smooth things over. Melissa Trevathan, the Christian counselor, often meets with clients who are asking some pretty big "why" questions, wondering if there could be any purpose to what's going on in their lives. She believes that, even if we had answers, they probably wouldn't satisfy us.

The central issue, she suggests, is trust. Can we

trust a God who seems to be absent in our time of need? Who allows tragedy to occur? Who leaves our desires unfulfilled?

Is it possible to see God as loving in spite of our circumstances? As present in spite of the loneliness we sometimes feel? As dependable when everything seems to be falling apart around us? Some people have been able to do so. Take Joseph, for instance.

WHERE ARE YOU, GOD?

Maybe he was naïve, a little loose with his mouth, a dreamer with the ability to interpret dreams. Joseph was his father's favorite son, which didn't score any points with his older brothers. When he told them he had a dream in which they bowed before him, that was the last straw.

His brothers sold him to slave traders and told their father that a wild animal killed him. Certainly an unexpected turn of events.

When Joseph arrived in Egypt, he was sold again and sent to serve in the house of Potiphar, one of the ruler's chief advisers. Because he was a handsome young man, Potiphar's wife tried to seduce him. He rejected her advances, so she told her husband that this Egyptian slave tried to rape her. Immediately he was thrown in prison with no hope of acquittal. Another unexpected path.

In prison Joseph met two of the king's servants, a cupbearer and a baker, who had also been incarcerated. They had mysterious dreams the same night and turned to Joseph to provide interpretations. Joseph told them the meaning of what they dreamed—the cupbearer would again serve in the king's palace, the baker would be executed. When the dreams came true, the cupbearer forgot his promise to plead Joseph's case before the king.

By then, Joseph must have thought he got a gigantic, bum deal. His only offense was being a bit obnoxious to his brothers, but that's hardly enough to merit watching his life drag by in a dungeon far from his homeland.

Two years passed before Joseph had any reason for hope. Then the king had a dream that no one in the court could interpret, and the cupbearer remembered the young Israelite. Because Joseph was able to explain the dream that predicted a disastrous famine, he was freed from prison and given growing responsibilities within the kingdom. In fact, he became second in command to the king—even though he was a foreigner.

When food became scarce throughout the land, Joseph's family came to Egypt in hopes of buying supplies. So much time had passed that his brothers didn't recognize him. Eventually, he revealed himself to them with these powerful words: "'Do not be afraid, for am I in the place of God? But as for you, you meant evil against me; but God meant it for good, in order to bring it about as it is this day, to save many people alive'... And he comforted them and spoke kindly to them" (Gen. 50:19–21 NKJV).

Joseph's comprehension of his purpose was amazing. He went through all these unexpected paths—years of hard times—before ultimately recognizing that these things happened so that millions of people, including his own family, could be saved from the famine.

Can you look at the unexpected paths in your life and accept the possibility that others could have meant things for evil but God meant them for good?

Looking for Good

Joseph's experience of interpreting those unexpected paths from God's viewpoint—"You meant it for evil, God used it for good"—occurs over and over again today for people like Maury Buchanan.

Growing up in a home with an angry, alcoholic father was tough for Maury. He never knew when his dad would erupt in a violent rage, abusing his mom or him verbally and physically. He wondered why his dad was that way and why his family seemed powerless to stop him. Maury remembers living with uncertainty on a daily basis.

In college, Maury became a Christian, which gave him hope and an eternal perspective—but still no answers to his "why" questions. Years passed before his dad would seek help and leave alcohol behind.

Today Maury is the director of Mission Discovery, a Christian organization that serves the poor in Mexico, Jamaica, and the Bahamas by offering short-term mission opportunities to teenagers and adults. He said that God has put things in perspective for him.

Growing up in a home where the unexpected could happen at any time was the perfect preparation for working in missions. When things don't go as planned (as is often the case when you're dealing with foreign governments), he takes it all in stride. His resourcefulness, calmness, and cheerfulness keep his staff, volunteers, and participants in good spirits as they go about their mission projects.

Almost fifteen years passed between the traumatic episodes in Maury's house and his realization that God was using these experiences for a reason. He is confident in telling people that God has a purpose for whatever they're going through . . . and he speaks with credibility.

Perhaps you haven't faced what Joseph or Maury did, but you've certainly encountered unexpected paths, some of which seemed disastrous at the time. What do you do with them? Relentlessly demand answers from God? Lose hope and walk away? Try to ignore what has happened? Or lean into them, even though things don't make sense, trusting God to be with you even when life is a mess?

Allow me to offer a few simple checkpoints. *First, examine your life for areas of sin that may have contributed directly to the problem.* If the Holy Spirit shines His light on anything, be quick to confess it and take whatever steps necessary to keep yourself from returning to the situation.

Second, if nothing comes to mind, pray for God to intervene in the situation and ask your friends or family members to pray for you. It's interesting to note that Job's life turned around when he prayed for his friends.

Third, if things don't seem to be changing for the better, ask God to give you grace to see you through these tough times. Through my involvement with the Make-A-Wish Foundation, I sometimes meet kids who have been diagnosed with illnesses that will prove fatal. That's never easy, knowing what lies ahead for them. Yet, I've met some courageous little kids who recognize their lives will be short, but they're absolutely sure God won't run out on them. They don't know why He doesn't heal them, but they know that He's ready to give them a great big hug as He welcomes them into heaven.

Fourth, be open to the possibility that God is preparing you to serve others. The song "Hello, Goodbye" on my album *Live the Life* was inspired by a little boy, Noah, who lived only two-and-a-half days because he was born with half a heart. It devastated me to think that I was holding that precious little life one day and the next day he was gone. His parents, Joey and Anne, were really sustained by prayer through those dark days.

Since then, they have been able to minister to people in similar circumstances in a way I can't begin to describe. I don't know why this happened, but I know they have chosen to let God use this tragedy to deepen their compassion to minister to others.

Perhaps no huge "whys" overshadow your heart. Your primary question may be "how?" How can you find God's purpose for your life? The next chapter offers some thoughts to consider.

TEN

FINDING YOUR PURPOSE

ith my busy schedule, reading is sometimes limited to the Bible, maybe a devotional book, and whatever my kids want their daddy to read to them. We own all the children's classics—*Winnie the Pooh*, Dr. Seuss, and *Alice's Adventures in Wonderland*. In the latter, author Lewis Carroll passes along some pretty heavy truth that seems appropriate here.

Poor Alice is overwhelmed by all that she's experiencing in this strange new land so she turns to the Cheshire Cat for advice:

> *"Would you tell me, please, which way I ought to go from here?"*
> *"That depends a good deal on where you*

want to get to," said the Cheshire Cat.
"I don't much care where—" said Alice.
"Then it doesn't much matter which way you
go," said the Cat.

For us as followers of Christ, it matters a great deal which way we go because we have a definite destination in mind. We have set forth on a journey. We are people who are valued by God and equipped with what we need to make it where we are bound. Isaiah 50:7 tells us: "The LORD God keeps me from being disgraced. / So I refuse to give up, / because I know God will never let me down" (CEV).

It's far easier to talk a good talk than to walk the walk. Even the devout prophet Elijah had his low moments. When we pick up his story in 1 Kings 19, he had just experienced a stellar victory. In a major showdown on Mt. Carmel, Elijah made it very clear to the Israelites that the pagan gods of Baal were no match for the Lord God. In a dramatic act of power, God sent fire from heaven to completely consume a sacrifice laid upon the altar. Then He sent rain to end a long drought.

The pagan priests, King Ahab, and Queen Jezebel were put to shame and the people got back on track spiritually. But Jezebel was one mean lady. She sent a message telling Elijah that he would be dead within twenty-four hours for the turmoil he caused in the kingdom.

After such a strong demonstration of faith, you'd expect him to respond with wisdom and confidence that would expose her wickedness. But what did Elijah do? He ran for his life!

He headed out into the wilderness where, distraught that he was like the faithless people he left behind, he prayed to die. God was merciful to this weary prophet and provided rest, food, and water for him.

Then God asked Elijah a question worthy of our consideration: "What are you doing here?" The prophet's response dramatically portrayed all that had occurred, with more than a hint of self-pity. It sounded as though Elijah questioned God's awareness of all that had happened. (Of course, no detail had slipped by Him.)

When the Lord asked him again, "What are you doing here?" he gave the same response. This time,

God instructed him to go back the way he came and bestow his responsibilities as prophet upon Elisha.

WHAT ARE YOU DOING HERE?

This question isn't meant to threaten you or make you defensive. You don't have to respond with complaints or excuses.

What has brought you to this point in your life? Where are you going from here? Let me try to help you get your bearings by asking a few questions:

Is there a verse that guides your thinking about life? Sometimes God establishes a little section of His Word deep within you that becomes a spiritual foundation upon which to build your life.

If you don't already have in mind a verse that will see you through life's storms, keep your eyes and heart open for a scripture that speaks to you in a personal way.

For example, you might connect with a verse like "I can do all things through Christ who strengthens me" (Phil. 4:13 NKJV). Or these directives from 1 Timothy 6:11–12: "Flee these things [areas of sins] and pursue righteousness, godliness, faith, love, patience, gentleness. Fight the good fight of faith, lay hold on eternal life, to which you were also called" (NKJV).

When you come across verses that speak to you, write them down, memorize them, and hide them in your heart to meditate on their meaning for your life.

What has brought true joy into your life so far? Look back over your life and identify those events and activities that seem to inspire your soul or encourage your heart. I'm not strictly speaking about the spiritual part of your life.

When I sit down at the piano, hours seem to pass in the blink of an eye. I feel totally connected to what I'm doing and, like Olympic runner Eric Liddell, I feel God's pleasure.

Maybe you're a baker and you love opening the oven to see your latest creation. Maybe you're into landscaping and God speaks to you through nature. Maybe you love to organize things so you feel great when you've stocked the shelves where you work or turned chaos into an office environment where everything has a proper place.

Identify what sort of activities seem to touch a

deep part of you and get creative about how you can direct those energies and abilities.

If you like studying problems until you come up with the right solution, maybe you'd make a good mechanic, doctor, or accountant. If you like juggling all sorts of possibilities until one seems best, maybe you belong in the arts, marketing, or engineering.

Ask your friends, family members, and coworkers to help you think things through. Their objectivity may prove valuable in your quest.

The more you get to know yourself, the more likely it is that you'll hone in on the purposes that ring true for your life. They may guide you toward a career or to a component that you could build into your free time.

For example, if you love kids, maybe you should become a teacher or a daycare worker. If that's not to be your job, it can still be your joy as you volunteer in your church's nursery.

How can you best honor God? You don't have to become a missionary or minister to give a right answer. Most of us aren't "professional Christians."

Let's say you're a construction worker. If you're honest, dependable, never give anything less than your best throughout the day, and are always "ready to give an answer when someone asks you about your hope" (1 Peter 3:15b CEV), you've found a great way to honor God with your life.

If you work in an office with a gracious and gentle attitude that makes you approachable to those whose lives aren't built on a strong foundation, you're honoring God.

Sometimes work may not be incredibly fulfilling, and you may not be thrilled by your surroundings or the monotony of daily activities. Nevertheless, give it all you've got, because you've been given eyes to see God's grander view and act in a way that honors Him.

As you continue to discover more about who you are, I pray this blessing for you: "May He grant you according to your heart's desire, / And fulfill all your purpose" (Ps. 20:4 NKJV).

PART 3

PASSION

The fire inside that
keeps us fully alive—
instead of merely existing

ELEVEN

HOLY FIRE

assion. The word has been tainted with overtly sexual images of soap operas, music videos, and lyrics that substitute cheap sensuality for genuine relationships. Think about how the word is being used these days and maybe you'll hear the seductive voice of a television announcer: "On tonight's world premiere movie, a story of passion and deceit . . ." You get the picture.

The word *passion* can also be defined as desire or urge. That's something we may know too much about. Almost every week we see on the news that a politician or celebrity's sexual misconduct has managed to become a headline story. Sadly, their first move is to hire an attorney or media spin doctor instead of taking the biblical (and simpler) approach of admitting wrongdoing, asking forgiveness, and starting over with a clean slate.

The apostle Paul warned the church in Galatia with these words:

> People's desires make them give in to immoral ways, filthy thoughts, and shameful deeds. They worship idols, practice witchcraft, hate others, and are hard to get along with. People become jealous, angry, and selfish. They not only argue and cause trouble, but they are envious. They get drunk, carry on at wild parties, and do other evil things as well. I told you before, and I am telling you again: No one who does these things will share in the blessings of God's kingdom. (5:19–21 CEV)

But Paul doesn't leave us stranded with just the negative aspects of our struggle with the flesh. He next portrays the godly desires that will transform us:

> God's Spirit makes us loving, happy, peaceful, patient, kind, good, faithful, gentle, and self-controlled. There is no

law against behaving in any of these
ways. And because we belong to Christ
Jesus, we have killed our selfish feelings
and desires. God's Spirit has given us life,
and so we should follow the Spirit. But
don't be conceited or make others jealous
by claiming to be better than they are.
(vv. 22–26, CEV)

The church has pretty much surrendered the
word *passion* to our culture instead of fighting for its
integrity. The only time it is used in a Christian setting
is during the planning of the Easter dramas we call
passion plays. The phrase has lost its meaning over
time, but that's what the story of Christ's life truly is—
a play of passion. It is scenes of the greatest story ever
told about the greatest man who ever lived.

PORTRAIT OF PASSION

Was Jesus passionate? Did Jesus merely exist? Or
did a fire inside Him keep Him fully alive? Picture
this scene from His life:

Jesus arrived at the temple where He found merchants set up inside the courtyard. He grabbed a whip and quickly drove them out, creating quite a commotion. Knowing that they wouldn't take such interference with their businesses without a fight, He cried out, "'Take these things away; stop making My Father's house a house of merchandise.' His disciples remembered that it was written, 'Zeal for thy house will consume me'" (John 2:16–17 NASB).

Zeal is not a word you hear much these days. You might find it in an old hymn or hear on the evening news that political zealots have created an uprising in some country, but that's about it.

Zeal is the King James word for passion and can also be translated as eagerness or desire. The imagery from the original Greek word conveys a flame burning up a candle. The picture that Scripture portrays of Jesus in the temple was: "The passion that I have for God will eat Me alive!"

He was stirred by a holy fire inside that could not be contained. Whatever word your Bible uses, be sure to note the emotion being conveyed.

Such passion is a long way from the polite,

timid faith that we see in many churches on Sunday morning. We have worked hard to make Christianity reputable and socially acceptable, rather than a holy fire. Somehow that image clashes with the real life of a man who was born in a barn, spent a lot of time hanging out with working class people, befriended people who would make most of us nervous, and died the death of a criminal.

Cross of Gold

Crosses today are pieces of fashionable jewelry instead of a reminder of One who suffered with nails in His hands and a crown of thorns on His head. Imagine how unnerving it would be to see someone wearing a little golden electric chair on a chain. That's a pretty fair correlation to what a cross meant two thousand years ago.

Perhaps you've seen the illustration where someone asks the question, "How much does Jesus love us?" The answer is spoken as arms are outstretched as though ready to be crucified: "This much."

That Holy Fire

Sometimes passion is bursting with visible trademarks.

Let me give you three brief examples of people who were definitely on fire for God.

When the ark was being escorted into Jerusalem, David danced before the Lord with all his might (2 Sam. 6:14). In fact, he was leaping and whirling with such abandon that Saul's daughter, Michal, was appalled by what she saw.

John the Baptist was a seriously different fellow, a man who wore clothes made of camel's hair and whose diet consisted of grasshoppers and honey. As a forerunner for Jesus, he was unparalleled in his passion and courage, freely telling everyone it was time to get their acts together because the Lord was coming. Many responded to his impassioned cries for repentance while he scorched the Pharisees and Sadducees with words of rebuke. He was fearless—even to the point of being beheaded after criticizing the king for marrying his brother's wife.

Apparently Paul and Silas were pretty intense in their worship while locked up in a Philippian jail, because as they prayed and sang, an earthquake shook the place so violently the doors opened and the chains fell off all the prisoners.

But don't think that we have to turn to ancient history to see genuine passion. Right now people in other parts of the world are taking a lot of heat for their beliefs. They're like Shadrach, Meshach, and Abednego being sent into King Nebuchadnezzar's blazing furnace because they refused to exalt anyone above God. These brothers and sisters in Christ fight the fires of persecution with the holy fire of faith inside. So did the late Christian singer Rich Mullins.

REMEMBERING RICH

Rich had an unusual gift for kindling the fires within people. Sometimes he said things to "stir up love and good works" (Heb. 10:24 NKJV), moving them to consider how they could walk more closely with God. And sometimes he just seemed to stir people up, sparking controversy with the things he said.

On the subject of passion, he often quoted Martin Luther who said, "Sin boldly." Then, he would slide in this chiding example based on President Clinton's admission that he had smoked marijuana but he hadn't inhaled. "If you're going to smoke marijuana," Rich would say in his warm but cranky way, "go ahead and inhale. Don't try to get off on technicalities. Know that you've done what you've done. If you're going to screw up, really screw up so when the grace of God comes into your life, you'll know that you've been saved in a big way."

Once the reality of grace has burned its indelible mark into our souls, we're called to action.

The book of Revelation is very clear about the importance of having a holy fire raging within us. In characterizing the church of Laodicea, the Lord says, "I know all the things you do, that you are neither hot nor cold. I wish you were one or the other! But since you are like lukewarm water, I will spit you out of my mouth! . . . I am the one who corrects and disciplines everyone I love. Be diligent and turn from your indifference" (3:15–16, 19 NLT). The Lord is saying, "Get fired up! There's no room for ho-hum living! Or for merely existing!"

But our lives are not supposed to be wildfires burning recklessly out of control. No, our flames are focused, purposeful, like a welder's torch. They don't blaze for the sake of experiencing tingly feelings.

Now, we'll look at the focus of our flame.

TWELVE

FOCUS OF
THE FLAME

hen I first started performing as a solo artist, audiences went nuts. No, it certainly wasn't because I was so great. It was because I wouldn't stand still. People almost got motion sickness watching me run from one side of the stage to the other.

I've always been pretty hyper, but that wasn't the reason I moved back and forth like a super-charged target in an arcade shooting gallery. The truth is this: I was nervous. The more tense I was, the faster I went.

Finally, my manager (and a few hundred of my closest friends) told me, "Smitty, you've got to slow down!" Instead of my movement making the show more exciting, it was distracting from the music.

Being energetic is important to presenting a good concert. Being out of control is not.

To solve my hyperactivity problem, people encouraged me to spend more time playing keyboards until I got used to performing live. Reciting Psalm 139 during concerts on the Friends tour was a way I developed to slow myself down and get a message across without becoming nervous. I also got a little coaching from people who helped me be a better communicator instead of a tornado with a wireless microphone.

We all need to keep a holy, purposeful focus to our passion.

KEEP YOUR FOCUS

Back in science class, I learned that you could use a magnifying glass on a sunny day to create enough heat to burn a hole in paper. The key was concentrating all the energy on a single point.

In *The Message* Eugene Peterson came up with a great way to express the Christian's response to this principle in Hebrews 12:

Keep your eyes on Jesus, who both began and finished this race we're in. Study how he did it. Because he never lost sight of where he was headed—that exhilarating finish in and with God—he could put up with anything along the way: cross, shame, whatever. And now he's there, in the place of honor, right alongside God. When you find yourselves flagging in your faith, go over that story again, item by item, that long litany of hostility he plowed through. That will shoot adrenaline into your souls! (vv. 2–3)

It's easy to get distracted. We're like Martha when Jesus came to visit. She busily tried to be a good hostess while her sister, Mary, listened at Jesus' feet. When she finally asked the Lord to make Mary help her, Jesus replied, "Martha, Martha, you are worried and troubled about many things. But one thing is needed, and Mary has chosen that good part, which will not be taken away from her" (Luke 10:41b–42 NKJV).

My updated translation is this: "Slow down,

Martha. You're running around like a maniac. Sit down and listen. You're missing out on what matters here." I need to hear those words, and maybe you do too.

Occasionally, I have so much on my schedule that I'm basically out of control. I can't concentrate on what's before me because I'm thinking about what I just finished and what lies ahead. It's a pretty crazy way to live—and when things get like that, I just lose it.

I find myself wanting to escape to my favorite hideaway in Colorado where I can spend time in solitude and get with God. I feel like a wrung-out sponge, dry and crushed, and I desperately need the Father to pour out His peace and joy on me to fill me up again.

Sometimes I can work Colorado into my schedule; other times I try to experience personal revival by driving in the country or walking around the farm. In those times of solitude God puts my priorities back in order, He reminds me of my purpose, and refuels me with what I need to follow Him with passion.

TAKE TIME TO REFUEL

Do you know Jesus' story of the ten virgins found in Matthew 25? It's a parable about being prepared for Christ's coming kingdom. Five young women brought extra oil for their lamps so they were ready when the bridegroom showed up for the wedding celebration. The other five realized they were running out of oil and hurried back to town to get an additional supply. By the time they returned, the celebration was under way and they were locked out.

Preachers who talk about this parable typically zero in on the idea of being locked out, but I want to emphasize the preparedness of the five wise women. They were ready for the long haul. They were prepared to go the distance. They had a holy, purposeful focus. They were marathon runners, not sprinters.

Suppose someone told you that he was planning to go on a hundred mile hike with an innovative plan. To keep from carrying the weight of food in his pack, he was going to eat four days' worth of meals just before heading into the woods. You would probably shake your head in disbelief because you know that he would need to reenergize as he went along.

Spiritually, we face the same situation. Some people try to live for years on a spiritual high from five or fifty years ago. Maybe you had a great experience at church camp that has been the sole source for sustaining your faith. Perhaps you had a significant encounter with God at a revival or retreat years ago but your soul hasn't received much nourishment since then. Let me be blunt—that's not enough to keep you going. You need to refuel on a regular basis.

Remember the story of God providing manna in the wilderness (Ex. 16)? Every morning (except on the Sabbath), the Israelites got up and found the ground blanketed with a flaky substance that could be used to make bread. They didn't have to do anything but collect it each day. Yet, it would sustain them as they went about their tasks. But when they tried to store up several days' supply of manna, it became infested with maggots.

In the same way, we must look to God to provide what we need each day. There's probably a good reason that the Lord's Prayer contains the phrase "give us today our *daily* bread" (Matt. 6:11). If we rely on Him with such regularity, we won't wander off like clueless sheep straying from our Shepherd. We'll stay in close relationship, deepening in our faith, growing in our ability to discern His voice, gaining new insights that help us make wise decisions about how to live our lives. We'll have His holy focus.

No one I know better exemplified that daily walk with God than a man my kids called Boompop.

A Lifetime of Love

A.V. Washburn was Debbie's grandfather, her mom's dad. He worked for years as the general secretary of the Southern Baptist Sunday School Board. His position involved preparation of curriculum, so he spent a lot of time visiting churches all over the country. Deb says that every Baptist knew his name. He had a purposeful, holy focus.

Boompop was one of the warmest, most encouraging people I've ever met. The kind of man who never met a stranger, he had a smile and a hug for everyone he met.

Deb was nine when her parents divorced and her grandfather became like a father to her. He was the stabilizing force in the family, the lap she could always crawl into, the one who always had time to listen. As the family expanded, he was the first to welcome newcomers. He took as much delight in his great-grandkids as his own children.

Whenever I played him a new song, he'd swing his fist in a playful uppercut and tell me, "That's going right to the top of the charts." He knew nothing about the music business but he was an expert at touching lives.

Even as he grew older, he refused to grow old. After retiring from the Sunday School Board, he and Kate became missionaries to Scotland for three years. He continued to burn with a purposeful, holy fire to serve His Lord.

Perhaps one of his greatest character traits was that he never stopped learning. Even up until his final days, he was set on growing in his knowledge of God and loving people better. His prayers were amazing, becoming deeper and more passionate as time went on.

When he died in December of 1997 at age

eighty-five, he left a legacy for his children, grand-children, and great-grandchildren. He dealt with hard times by holding on to Jesus with all his strength. He faced cancer twice in his life without becoming bitter or withdrawn. He boldly lived out his faith with a naturalness that captivated everyone he met and greeted each day with an enthusiasm that I want to embrace. He truly had a holy, pur-poseful focus. So does my friend Michael Guido.

A WILD MAN of FAITH

Just as John the Baptist was an unconventional leader, Michael Guido is a man of passionate faith (although quite different from Boompop). Guido is sort of a freelance pastor to artists in Christian music and their families, but he is also a relentless evangelist.

A few years ago, we were backstage preparing for a concert at a theatre in Pittsburgh, Pennsylvania, the Syria Mosque. My manager Chaz Corzine offhandedly suggested to Guido that he should share the Lord with this enormous, tough-looking guy who was hanging out behind the auditorium.

Guido's standard philosophy is that you earn the right to share your faith as you build relationships, and since we were in town for only a few hours, there wasn't time for that slower approach. To Chaz's surprise, Guido jumped up and headed for the loading dock where we had seen this fellow.

And Guido believes the Holy Spirit jump-started this conversation for him. "What's the concert about?" the guy asked casually. Immediately, Guido was given an open door to talk about Christian music.

"The building isn't Christian," he told the huge man, "but Jesus is here tonight." Guido explained who Jesus was and how much He loved this very intimidating guy.

Eventually Guido came to a point where he felt he was supposed to ask the guy for a commitment. "This is an opportunity for you to receive Christ. Do you want to take Him up on His offer based on what He did on the cross for you?"

The man prayed a sinner's prayer and walked away from that encounter quite different than he had been an hour earlier. Chaz and I learned a great lesson in Guido's example of boldness and his focused, holy purpose for this man.

"John 3 tells us that we're like the wind," Guido said. "We don't necessarily know where we're going. Abraham didn't know where he was going, but he followed faithfully.

"Unfortunately, we want to know where we're going all the time," he added. "In fact, we'll even tell God where we're going." Obviously such an attitude will get us into trouble every time. We have to be available at any time for God to direct us as He sees fit. That's an "eye exam" to check whether our focus is correct.

Everything that blocks a reverent view of God has to topple—our careers, our dreams, our friendships. All of them have to submit to God's overwhelming call on our lives. We have to have that holy, purposeful focus.

May God's purposeful passion leave its mark on you and those around you. However, that may not happen as you expect. Sometimes holy passion is expressed in very ordinary ways.

THIRTEEN

THE GREAT
AND THE HARDLY
NOTICEABLE

hen I first moved to Nashville, my
thinking was almost schizophrenic.
Some days I felt I was getting ready
to take the music business by storm.
I was sure I would get discovered by some record
mogul, and in a year my name would be right up
there next to Elton John and Billy Joel. Other days I
was just hoping that a local publisher would hear
my music and like what he heard—and maybe I
would be able to make a living as a musician. On
dark days I questioned whether I had much of anything to offer anybody.

Over time, I gravitated somewhere toward a
middle ground—neither overly confident nor
despairing, neither overly optimistic nor pessimistic.

Sometimes we confuse passion with doing great things. Look at most of the great leaders through history and the heroes in movies. You see people who are doing and saying things that make them seem bigger than life. We don't know that much about the lives of average people precisely because they're average people.

The truth is that the vast majority of people are just ordinary folks. Even Billy Graham, the best known and most respected Christian leader of our time, regards himself as simply a country preacher. But most of us think average isn't all that good.

Do you remember the story of the rich young ruler who came to see Jesus? He asked: "Good Teacher, what good thing shall I do that I may have eternal life?" (Matt. 19:16 NKJV). The guy must have been quite sincere, or really polite, since he's the only person in the whole New Testament who called Jesus not just Teacher (or Rabbi) but Good Teacher. Maybe he was trying to score points with Jesus, to flatter Him. If so, he would come to realize that would never work.

Jesus responded, as He so often does, with a question: "Why do you call Me good? No one is good but One, that is, God. But if you want to enter into life, keep the commandments" (v. 17 NKJV).

We weren't given the young man's answer to Jesus' inquiry. But he seemed interested in seeing how high he ranked in spirituality. "Which commandments?" he asked.

The Lord answered by mentioning some of the Ten Commandments, those that involve treating people morally and ethically. "You shall not murder, You shall not commit adultery, You shall not steal, You shall not bear false witness, Honor your father and your mother."

The man was probably feeling pretty good about himself by then. He said, "All these things I have kept from my youth." Then he added a question that changed everything: "What do I still lack?" (v. 20 NKJV).

Maybe he expected Jesus to say, "Build a building in My honor, or write down My teachings so My words can be presented to the local philosophers, or establish a scholarship at the synagogue in My name." He was probably ready to do anything that had an air of nobility about it.

Jesus' response called his bluff: "If you want to

be perfect, go, sell what you have and give to the poor, and you will have treasure in heaven; and come, follow Me" (v. 21 NKJV).

The young ruler didn't expect this answer. Suddenly, he got very quiet because, Scripture tells us, he had great wealth. We are told that he went away sorrowful. It's not hard to imagine that he rode up to Jesus with great fanfare, ready to prove his virtue. But he left silently, his eyes cast down, because Jesus touched the core of his being and asked the man to sacrifice and be obedient.

We're sometimes like that ruler in two ways. In the first place, we don't want to give up something that we hold dear. Something in our soul tells us that the price of true discipleship is too much. The Lord may be telling us to give up a friendship, a habit, a dating relationship, or a lifestyle in order to truly follow Him. It's a message that we need to be reminded of frequently, especially since we're living in crazy times where the idea of submitting to God stands in radical conflict with our culture.

The second message isn't quite so obvious. How many times have you heard someone talk about wanting to do some great thing for God? You watch television evangelists unveiling gigantic plans for new projects costing enormous amounts of money. A growing church decides that it needs to build the largest sanctuary in town. A concert sponsor steps beyond realism, claiming that the music will forever change the lives of everyone who comes. (I wince thinking about those who make such grandiose promises.)

Do you know that you don't have to do anything earth-shattering to be a world changer for God? Unless you happened to read the dedication on my *Live the Life* album, you probably would have never heard of Boompop, yet he made a difference everywhere he went. My parents have never made the cover of magazines or been interviewed by network news crews but they have tremendous influence within their community and their church. The staff and volunteers at our Rocketown ministry are not famous but they're changing the lives of teenagers and young adults.

I think we need a new definition of greatness. It's not how big or how prominent or how successful something is. Instead, something is great if it involves a person being obedient. One more child gets a Compassion International sponsor. A young adult finds a mentor. A couple opens their home, inviting the teenagers in the community to stop by anytime they'd like to talk about something.

Maybe it's not so great in scope. Not flashy. Not even newsworthy. Hardly even noticeable. Yet, God's kingdom purposes are being accomplished. That is truly purposeful, holy passion.

AND SOMETIMES GREAT
IS GREAT BIG

Before you think I'm against anything big, let me say that we serve a big God who does indeed do big things. My experience, however, has been that usually those big things come after people have been proven faithful in small things.

The guys in Jars of Clay had no idea how quickly they would become well-known, selling lots of records, getting a lot of mainstream exposure, having their songs on movie soundtracks, opening for Sting. The wonderful thing about them was that they were excited about simply having the opportunity to play music. They were happy to be a college band who could pay their bills.

Billy Graham never needed to fill stadiums to satisfy an inflated ego. Numbers were always secondary to the impact a crusade had on a community. Even though he has accomplished so much in his life, he remains unbelievably humble. He's known around the world as a man of God, yet he brushes aside any praise.

Not too long ago, I performed prior to his speaking at a youth crusade in Canada. He leaned over to me during the program and said, "The people wouldn't be here except for you." I know better. I know people are drawn to hear the simple messages he drives home with such passion and compassion.

In the past few years, his son, Franklin, has become a friend. The organization he leads, Samaritan's Purse, has become one of the most expansive mission organizations in the world since its formation in 1970. When disaster strikes in the form of hurricanes, famines, or civil war, Samaritan's Purse is on the scene. Whenever there is poverty or distress, Franklin's staff takes holy, purposeful action.

As I look at my own life, God has taken me to places far beyond my wildest dreams growing up in Kenova, West Virginia. Setting aside milestones relating to my career, I think about traveling to Ecuador several times on mission trips to see our Compassion daughters Gavi and Ximena, hearing songs I've written sung in churches (including a few that are actually in hymnals), and having the opportunity to get to know people like the Grahams. Sometimes God lets us express our holy passion in great big ways.

What is the Lord asking of you? If it's to do something great for His kingdom, prepare well and go after it. But I'm absolutely sure God is asking us to do the not-so-great things every day. Our willingness to do them—to daily pick up our cross and follow Jesus where He leads us—is our fulfillment of the holy purpose at hand and possibly our preparation for bigger things to come.

Clean up your room. Write that letter. Call that friend. Memorize those verses. Bake some cookies and take them to a neighbor. Spend some time covering your family with prayer. Do the boring task at church that no one wants to tackle. Pay attention to someone who gets overlooked. Practice your musical instrument. Do whatever it is that the Holy Spirit is moving you toward.

These activities may not live up to the dramatic notions of passionate living, yet they're like blocks that form the foundation on which you can build your life.

But what do you do if that fire within has nearly been extinguished? Let's look at what may be missing.

FOURTEEN

REKINDLING
THE FLAME

hen I was in high school, most of my closest friends were several years older than me. Several were fellow church members. By the time I reached my junior year, they were away at college or off on their own. Most maintained a strong relationship with the Lord but some didn't. They left our small town and got caught up in things that were contrary to the way we were raised.

At the time, I was on fire for God and pretty idealistic. I just couldn't believe they could get sidetracked. I thought about all the great times we'd shared—the church youth musicals, the trips, the fellowship times, the impromptu prayer meetings at our house.

How could they walk away from the things they knew to be true?

Then I moved away from Kenova, West Virginia, and fell into some of the same pits. While playing in bar bands in Nashville, I lived in a series of pretty crummy places. In those days, my parents made frequent trips to see me. My mom, bless her heart, would bring her sewing machine and sew curtains to try to make whatever dump I was living in seem a little more like home.

Spiritually, I was in some pretty crummy places too. I was a total night owl, playing in a Holiday Inn lounge until two or three in the morning, then sleeping most of the day. The people I hung around with were hardly encouraging. In fact, one of my roommates sold drugs.

During those dark days, the flame of my faith was barely flickering, and I was doing nothing to fuel it. My family and friends back home had some understanding of what was going on in my life but they knew that as an adult I had to make my own decisions. I'm sure their thoughts were similar to the ones I had had only a few years before about my friends who had gone astray.

Wayne Kirkpatrick did an incredible job of capturing those feelings in the song "I Miss the Way" from my album, *i2eye*.

Once a true believer
Once there was a fire in your soul
You were the epitome of blessed faith astir
With thirst for holiness
And hunger for the Word
Now you move in other circles
To the beat of different drums
And I see only glimpses of the one you
used to be
The inspiration that you were to me

I miss the way His love would dance
within your eyes
I miss the way His heart was the soul
of your life
And somewhere in the saddest part of
heaven's room
Our Father sheds a tear for you
He's missing you too[1]

Things turned around for me when I crashed from a bad experience with drugs and realized just how desperately I needed God. I totally relate to David's words in Psalm 34:17: "The righteous cry out, and the LORD hears, / And delivers them out of all their troubles. / The LORD is near to those who have a broken heart, / And saves such as have a contrite spirit" (NKJV).

Within a few months of bottoming out, the Lord opened the door for me to leave the bar band and begin traveling with the Christian group Higher Ground. He started rekindling the fire of faith within me.

SEARCHING FOR THAT
MISSING PERSON

I get letters all the time from people who relate to my story and to the songs that portray these feelings. Many have seen their passion for God turn to passive church attendance, and others have just given up on what they know to be true.

Maybe it's been years since you opened the Bible and felt like God wrote some verses especially for you. Maybe your prayer time is more of a habit than an opportunity to pour out your heart to God. Or maybe you've given up on praying altogether.

As the song on my album *Live the Life* suggests, it's time you started searching for that "Missing Person."

> *Under a lavender moon*
> *So many thoughts consume me*
> *Who dimmed the glowing light*
> *That once burned so bright in me*
> *Is this a radical phase*
> *A problematical age*
> *That keeps me running from all that*
>   *I used to be*
> *Is there a way to return*
> *Is there a way to unlearn*
> *That carnal knowledge*
> *That's chipping away at my soul*
> *Have I been gone too long*
> *Will I ever find my way home* [2]

The answer to that last question is a definite yes! But where do you start?

Remember the story of Elijah we visited in Chapter 5? After he ran for his life from Queen Jezebel, he sank into a deep depression. God revived him with food, water, and sleep, then sent him on his way with these words: "Go back the way you came."

Sometimes the best way to move forward is go back the way you came. Remember those key moments in your life when you knew without a doubt that God was directing you.

Some people call these times Ebenezers based on a story in 1 Samuel 7. It details how God protected His people when their enemies were about to attack. He caused tremendous thunder, confusing the army so thoroughly the soldiers were easily routed by the Israelites. The prophet Samuel set up a large stone as a monument and called it Ebenezer, which means "thus far the Lord has helped us."

Go back and remember your own Ebenezers, those times when you know God was at work in your life. Can you recall a prayer that was answered just in the nick of time? A time when you knew such incredible peace and joy that it must have been caused by God? Something happened that can only be described as a miracle? A Bible verse that spoke loud and clear about a specific situation you were facing?

As you bring those things to mind, they will be like tiny pieces of kindling on the flicker of a fire.

The more you remember, the more you feed the flame. With the loving support of other believers, the flame grows more brilliant. Then all you need to do is to keep that holy passion burning.

Let's consider now how brightly that candle burns within you.

FIFTEEN

Keep the flame Burning

ne of the unexpected perks of marrying Debbie is that her stepfather, Murray Severance, frequently serves as a guide on chartered trips to Israel.

On two occasions, Deb and I have joined his tour. When you get out in the open country, you see shepherds tending their flocks just like they did two thousand years ago. Some of the countryside is pretty barren, a far cry from the green hills of Tennessee.

In the Israeli wilderness, trees are notable just because they manage to survive. Even a scrubby bush of any size attracts attention. Imagine how quickly your eye would be drawn to a bush that was fully ablaze.

That's exactly what Moses saw in the distance

and felt compelled to get a closer look. When he drew near, he noticed that bush wasn't just burning—it was burning without being consumed. What an awe-inspiring sight!

Why wasn't it going up in smoke? Because God was there in its midst. Exodus 3:4 says, "God called to him from the midst of the bush and said, 'Moses, Moses!'" (NKJV).

The guy must've been completely tripping! Not only did he see this mysterious phenomenon, God called him by name as he came closer. It was no accident that Moses passed that way or that he was drawn to holy ground to accept a mission from God. It was a divine encounter that would change his life forever.

Now let's talk about you. Take the following inventory of your holy passion:

Is God in the Midst of the Fires in Your Life?
Don't answer too quickly. Don't be defensive or too quick to discount the value of things that may not appear very spiritual at first glance.

Cooking, playing the piano, climbing a mountain—none of these activities is laid out in the Bible as essential for spiritual maturity. Yet, God can speak to a person through any of these.

Can you find a way to connect your passions to the One who created us? If you love to cook, can you honor God by using your skills as a hospitable host or hostess? If you're a musician, do you praise the One who made music in the first place? If you're into climbing, do you marvel at the many awesome works of nature that He created?

If you have a hard time connecting your passions to God, it may be worth your time to question why they are important to you. Do they serve any positive purpose (including recreation or building relationships) or are they merely fortresses for self-indulgence? Don't be too hard on yourself but don't be afraid to consider the question.

How Would You Gauge Your Temperature?
Remember in Revelation 3 where the Lord tells the church that He wishes they were either hot or cold?

Put your passion for God on a scale of 1 to 10. Where are you now? What's the "hottest" you've been? What's the "coldest"? What has caused the fluctuation?

How does passion express itself through you? Is your life characterized by the quiet steadiness of Boompop or by the bold directness of Guido? Is there another way that you communicate your passion? Maybe you can't stop talking about what excites you, or you find ways to tie virtually any part of your life to your passion. It's worthwhile to know how you express your passion. It'll also provide a sensitive warning signal to know when your passion seems to fade.

Do You Equate Passion with Anger?

Many people equate passion with an issue. Usually that means something that has incurred their wrath. They're upset about taxes, drunk driving, child abuse, Native American land rights, government intervention in the lives of citizens, or some other issue.

Keep in mind that godly passion doesn't just burn—it burns for a kingdom purpose. When Jesus raised a ruckus in the temple, it was because He was furious that people were turning his Father's house into a den of thieves. He wasn't just mad to be mad. And even in His fury, His accusations were intended to send a wake-up call to their souls.

Godly passion is like that. It goes beyond anger to a greater purpose.

It doesn't just stand against pornography; it seeks to heal those who are being abused by it and to rescue those who are addicted to its damaging effects.

It doesn't just hate abortion; it grieves for the babies lost, for the women who believe that it's the only choice they have, and for medical professionals who don't fully understand the value of human life. It wants to come alongside and administer grace instead of shouting accusations from a distance.

It doesn't just rail against homosexuality; it brims with compassion for those who struggle with desires they may not fully understand. It seeks to restore the individuals instead of merely condemning the sin.

How Do You Stoke the Fires of Your Passion?
It's highly unlikely that it will happen by accident. Instead, it's an act of the will, a choice you make, a discipline that you acquire.

There are some practical steps you can take to add more fuel to your fire.

1. *Realize how important fellowship is to your spiritual growth.* Jonathan and David were close friends who kept each other encouraged. Paul frequently traveled with one or more of the other disciples to support him spiritually and emotionally.

2. *Seek out accountability—not just fellowship.* When you're living like a Lone Ranger, sin can worm its way into your life. You need the honesty and openness of true Christian friends to confess your areas of struggle and receive their prayers for freedom and forgiveness.

3. *Experience worship as part of your daily life.* You don't have to be in a group to worship. It doesn't require a guitar or a piano or a hymnal. Simply open your heart in praise to God. As you empty yourself in worship, you'll be amazed at how He fills you up.

"Let the word of Christ dwell in you richly in all wisdom, teaching and admonishing one another in psalms and hymns and spiritual songs, singing with grace in your hearts to the Lord" (Col. 3:16 NKJV).

4. *Get into the Word.* I truly believe that God can speak fresh words to our hearts, but He is always speaking to us through the Bible. If you're not feeding on God's Word, you're missing out on nourishment you need—and possibly missing out on gaining new insights.

5. *Call to mind the times that you recognize the Lord's faithfulness.* Repeat those events to yourself just as David did:

> I will remember the works of the LORD;
> Surely I will remember Your wonders
>   of old.
> I will also meditate on all Your work,
> And talk of Your deeds. (Ps. 77:11–12
> NKJV)

6. *What if you have no passions?* It's sad but true that many people live life without becoming very enthusiastic about anything. "The great tragedy of today's convenient world is that you can live a trivial life and get away with it," writes speaker and author Tim Hansel in his book *Holy Sweat*.[1] He's right!

Far too many people spend much of their time being bored and complaining about how boring boredom is. It's time to drop the remote control and get off the couch.

Go on a quest to find what stirs your soul. Rev up your curiosity. Go to a good bookstore and browse magazines beyond your normal choices to see if you find anything interesting. Read biographies about people who were passionate about living. Make a list of your heroes and write down why they inspire you. Talk to others about what fires are ignited within them. Let their enthusiasm for life prove contagious, moving you from information-seeking to action.

7. *Are you taking risks?* No, I'm not talking about irresponsible thrills like speeding. Do something that requires guts, not stupidity.

Audition for a play or musical group. Get involved in a ministry on the edge like those that serve AIDS patients or street kids. Form a small group of Christians who will commit to be completely honest and accountable to one another. Follow through on an interest you've always said that you'd like to explore one day. Step outside your comfort zone with an activity that requires increasing your physical endurance such as hiking or running. Share your faith with a friend who is not a Christian.

Taking positive risks will almost automatically drive you to prayer. When you stay in the safety zone, you feel like you can take care of yourself but when you step outside yourself, you'll instantly feel the need for the Lord's protection, guidance, and courage.

When we risk, we place ourselves more boldly into God's hands, and that deliberate decision stirs the coals of passion within.

As we move out in confidence, we begin to see God's plan unfolding in our lives. That's just what we'll begin to consider in part four.

PART 4

GOD'S
PLAN

A review of our journey
so far—and a look ahead
at what the Lord may
have in store

SIXTEEN

DISTANT DRUMS

lmost every Friday night from September through November, I heard drums in the distance from my family's home. I would put on my green and white cap and pace anxiously across the front yard, wanting my mom, dad, and sister to hurry. Our destination: the Ceredo-Kenova High School football stadium.

The whole town would show up for games, and excitement always filled the air. The drums pounded relentlessly, the great smells of food from the concession stand swirled in the breeze, and the bright, white lights high above us would make the whole setting seem like a dream.

In those days, I had a major crush on a majorette who was older than me. She'd be standing in front of the home seats, wearing her green and white outfit with the cool trim and big buttons. I'd be sitting in the stands, a goofy grin on my face. But it was a love that was never meant to be—probably because I was in the third grade at the time and she was pushing sixteen years old.

Once I reached high school age—after years in the stands—I was convinced I belonged on the field. I tried out and made the team as an end and extra point kicker.

It's not bragging to say that we had a great football program. Our team had an exceptional coaching staff and was a dominant force in the division. In fact, we were state champions my junior and senior years.

There was a brief period of time when I considered pursuing a career in football. Similarly, I had thought about playing professional baseball until I failed to make the all-star team when I was fourteen or fifteen years old. Even though I loved sports, my heart was never fully into either of them. It's like I was somehow holding out for the right thing to come along.

Long before my involvement in sports, I had shown an interest in music. I took up drums when I was six, then switched to piano a year later. My parents say they were really glad when I decided to make that change!

My grandmother began teaching me to play piano. I didn't have much patience for learning the technical parts of music but I was good at playing by ear. I could hear songs and know how to play them.

My mom loves to tell about the time when two ladies from church came over to visit. One always read Scripture and the other always prayed. After they had done so, I went over to the piano and played "Just As I Am" because I figured that we must be having a church service.

Even back then, my folks recognized that I might be gifted in music.

Through my teenage years, my love for piano grew. I was playing a lot at church and picking out songs that I loved—anything from Andrae Crouch to Billy Joel.

My folks weren't really sure how my aspirations might support me but they were supportive of my desires.

They encouraged me to get a music education in preparation for following my dreams, so I agreed to attend Marshall University in Huntington. I lasted one semester.

In my search for direction, my parents paid for me to attend the Christian Artists Seminar at Estes Park, Colorado. There I had the opportunity to talk with two of my heroes, singer/songwriters Randy Stonehill and Larry Norman. I came back home totally psyched that this was what I wanted to do with my life.

"If you're going to follow music, you can't do it here," Dad told me one day. That's when I decided to move to Nashville.

To support myself, I worked in all kinds of situations. One of those jobs was working at Coca-Cola back in the days when everything came in glass bottles. For a guy who hoped to make a living with his hands, working around glass was a dangerous activity but it proved a great motivator to succeed in music as quickly as possible.

The more I played, the more I wanted to record an album. My dad was the voice of reason: "Who's gonna buy it? You've only got so many friends." (Dad didn't know anything about the music business, but he and Mom were great about keeping my feet on the ground.)

My parents always prayed that my sister and I would grow up loving God and serving Him. They weren't sure how that service might be rendered but they were committed to keeping us on God's plan for our lives. As I've mentioned previously, sometimes I hung onto my faith by little more than a thread, but that tie was never severed.

All along I believed that God had a plan for me. It wasn't to pursue a career in professional sports and it wasn't playing drums. I believe with all my heart that it's what I'm doing today—writing songs, recording albums, performing, and writing books.

I was meant to travel to the beat of a different drummer—far from my hometown and far from any profession my family was familiar with.

I get letters from people who think that I've always had it figured out. Not so.

SEEING THE PIECES
COME TOGETHER

Have you ever looked back over a day, a year, or even a decade of your life and seen that God was at work? Maybe you thought that events seemed unrelated at the time but in retrospect, it was almost as though your life was a story with a theme, connected incidents, and a unifying conclusion.

You reflect and see how God provided a friend or finances or an insight at just the right time to make things work out. That's how I look at my life. Now I can gaze over my shoulder and see how God was putting together the pieces of His plan for me.

And it's not just my life. I think about how God allowed me to play a role in His plan of working in Chris Rodriguez's life in 1985.

After being introduced to him by guitarist Dann Huff, it seemed like everywhere I went around Nashville I ran into Chris Rodriguez. At the time, I was trying to pull together a band for the Friends tour. On several occasions, I had seen him but didn't see any handwriting on the wall. I remember asking, *God, why do I keep bumping into him?* When I asked the question, I got no answer. In fact, I wasn't even sure there was an answer.

We kept looking for band members, but we weren't coming up with a guitarist who really fit the bill. Finally, I thought I'd give Chris a try.

When he came over to the house, I liked him immediately, but his manner and appearance made me wonder if this guy was a pot smoker. His audition went well but I wasn't sure if I should ask him to join us on the road.

Obviously, pot smoking wasn't an option for someone I was going to employ, but I began to believe that God wanted him on the tour. From our conversation, I could tell that he wasn't a Christian.

Should we take the risk?

With time running out, I took a leap of faith and asked him to play guitar and sing background vocals. I was sure there was some reason that God had in mind—I just hoped things didn't blow up in my face.

About two weeks into the tour, Chris came to my dressing room before a concert with tears in his eyes and said, "I'm coming over to your side."

We hadn't been witnessing to him or putting on any pressure at all. He had just seen how the other guys in the band related to each other and how important a relationship with God meant to each of us. Right there, he accepted Christ with all the other guys gathered around. As it turned out, it was his birthday so we gave him a Bible to commemorate being born and being born again.

But God had more than salvation awaiting Chris on that road trip. When we played Eugene, Oregon, he met a girl named Lisa who was a big fan of my music. Romance hit them hard, and in six months they were married.

To this day, Chris has remained solid in his faith, with a career that includes recording sessions with dozens of Christian artists as well as performing for years in Kenny Loggins's band.

In retrospect, I believe God's plan was being followed. At the time, I was just going on a gut feeling that I really hoped was the leading of the Holy Spirit. As time proved, the other band members and I were meant to befriend Chris and lead him to Christ by our actions. We really do "walk by faith, not by sight" (2 Cor. 5:7 NKJV).

When we think about God's plan for our lives, our minds whirl with questions. How can we know His plan for us? How can we be sure we are following this plan?

The answers are all part of a much bigger picture.

Seventeen

THE BIG PICTURE
AND THE LITTLE
DETAILS

hen it comes down to it, what God wants for me is what He wants for you. He has the same big picture in mind for all of us. Simply stated, He just wants us to be His in every way. To look like Him.

Just as my sons, Ryan and Tyler, resemble me because we are genetically made up of the same DNA, our redemption into God's family means that we begin to look like Jesus in a spiritual sense.

How do we do this? We get rid of everything that keeps us from becoming more like Jesus—pride, lies, bitterness, lust, envy, secret sins. And we take hold of everything that will make us more like Him. we see the world through His eyes, listen to the Father as He did, treat people like He did.

That's exactly what Hebrews 12:1–2 tells us: "We must get rid of everything that slows us down, especially the sin that just won't let go. And we must be determined to run the race that is ahead of us. We must keep our eyes on Jesus, who leads us and makes our faith complete" (CEV).

As we see the big picture beginning to unfold, we will also see God at work in the small details.

THE LITTLE DETAILS

In the past few years, I've had some incredible opportunities to travel to faraway countries where the people's lives are so different from my own. In particular, my travels with Franklin Graham are always an adventure. The Christian equivalent of Indiana Jones, he is a man who believes in living life to its fullest. When he preaches, he gives it all he's got. When he plays, he is an absolute maniac.

In April 1997 I joined Franklin on a trip to Soweta, South Africa, where we distributed shoeboxes filled with toys to children in an orphanage. As we were working our way from room to room, we came upon a sweet faced girl no more than ten years old who was blind.

Now, you need to know something about these boxes we were delivering. They were among the hundreds of thousands that caring individuals had assembled using general guidelines provided by Samaritan's Purse. Each box packer has a degree of freedom in selecting the items he or she would like to include. A family may have picked out items for one box or a church may have met to create a hundred. The giver has no idea who the recipient will be.

I reached for a box and placed it in this little girl's hands. I told her that this was a gift from someone in the United States who loved Jesus and wanted to her to have a special present.

My heart almost stopped when I helped her open the box. Inside were a variety of items—almost all of which made noise. They were perfect gifts for a child who couldn't see. A note inside sent blessings from a family in California. It was my privilege to carry a message back to them that their gift was exactly right.

Now you could argue with me on this but I believe that God was involved in the details of this situation. Without their knowing it, I think He led this family in California to choose gifts that would bring real pleasure to a little blind girl in South Africa.

I supposed that I was randomly picking a box from those available but I knew as soon as I saw what was inside, I had connected with God's plan for that moment. Surely if He knows the number of hairs on our heads, it's not difficult for Him to sort through those thousands of boxes to find one that is perfect for each girl or boy.

I think God did a similar sorting job when it comes to my songwriting partners. He took care of all the details without my knowing it.

WAYNE KIRKPATRICK, LANDSCAPE ENGINEER

Over the years, no one has expressed my heart more than Wayne Kirkpatrick. Since first teaming with him in 1985, he has provided the lyrics for more than fifty songs on my albums.

Magazines have quoted me as saying that I

believe we were meant to write together, that God set that up before the foundations of the earth along with a few billion other details. But it didn't have to turn out that way.

For one thing, you need to know that there are hundreds, maybe even thousands, of songwriters in Nashville who are always working on new tunes. I could have ended up with any number of them but God allowed me the opportunity to collaborate with Wayne. I count that a wonderful gift. He can take even a vague idea and express my heart with eloquence and humor. (Who else could work "Mongolian barbecue" into a lyric as he did on "Love Me Good"?)

It's no wonder that he's had songs recorded by Amy Grant, Gary Chapman, Susan Ashton, Bruce Carroll, and Billy Sprague as well as Wynonna, Trisha Yearwood, and Kathy Mattea. He shares credit with Gordon Kennedy and Tommy Sims for "Change the World," recorded by Eric Clapton, which won the Grammy for Song of the Year in 1997.

But did you know that Wayne Kirkpatrick, songwriter extraordinaire, could have easily become Wayne Kirkpatrick, landscape engineer? It's true. He was three years into a five-year program at LSU when he decided to give songwriting a try. Because Baton Rouge seemed an unlikely place to make a living as a songwriter, he moved to Nashville and hasn't felt the need to go back and finish his degree. I think he's doing just fine where he is!

I'm sure that we could have survived without each other, but I think God was looking out for me when Wayne came along at just the right time.

Do you realize that you may be coming along at just the right time for someone?

TIMING IS EVERYTHING

Maybe you arrive on the scene just in time to calm a frantic child or give a shoulder for someone to cry on or help someone through a difficult situation. You may be the one who has a great idea that draws people into worship or helps raise money for a summer missions trip. Or you may help communicate the gospel to people who have never understood Christ's message.

Back when "Place in This World" was a hit, I had the chance to do a lot of mainstream publicity.

VH-1 invited me to host their video countdown show, so I flew to New York to spend a few hours at their studio. The makeup artist was extremely curious about where I was coming from spiritually. She kept saying, "There's something different about you." I couldn't imagine the door opening any wider so I told her, "I've got a relationship with Jesus Christ and it has totally changed my life."

You could say that sentence to some people and they would completely blow you off. She didn't. I could see that she connected with what I was saying. Her heart seemed ready to receive a little bit of the gospel so I said what God placed on my heart.

Similar situations unfolded frequently while "Place in This World" was riding high on the charts. I was constantly surrounded by people who were not Christians—agents, promoters, technical crew members at TV shows, and radio DJs. Many had some religious background and freely talked about how they had been burned by believers, how Christians were hypocritical, and how much they disliked organized religion.

I listened to them and simply said that Christ

had revolutionized my life. It's hard to argue with a changed life, and I think God used my interaction with so many mainstream people to plant seeds that I pray have been fed and watered by others.

Did it matter that I had a big hit? It certainly helped pay the bills, and I'll admit that it was a major rush emotionally. However, I think that the purpose of that big success was to have all those little conversations so I could place the hope of that song into the lives of people who were struggling. I came along at just the right time because I allowed God to take care of the little details.

A VERY PRESENT GOD

What are the details that concern you right now? Maybe you have a health problem. Maybe your family is going through a trying time. Maybe you're lonely. Maybe you're having a difficult time controlling your temper.

Whatever you're up against, know that God is present. He sees what you're going through—and He's paying close attention to how you respond to the pressure, the heartache, the fear, or the frustration.

He promised that "nothing can separate us from God's love—not life or death, not angels or spirits, not the present or the future, and not powers above or powers below. Nothing in all creation can separate us from God's love for us in Christ Jesus our Lord!" (Rom. 8:38–39 CEV).

Sometimes He provides quick responses to our questions. Sometimes those answers seem to take forever.

Do you remember the story of the fierce storm that threatened to capsize the boat Jesus and His disciples were traveling aboard (Mark 4:36–41)? While His followers were completely freaking out, Jesus was asleep on a cushion in the back of the boat. They woke Him and asked, "Don't you care that we're about to drown?" He got up and told the storm to be still. Immediately, it responded to His command. He turned to His disciples and said, "Why are you so scared? Don't you have faith?"

Sometimes the Lord brings a calming solution to the situations we face. Sometimes He rides out the storm with us. Both require faith, but the latter requires perseverance too.

That quality builds over time just as a runner gains endurance as he trains. Romans 5:4–5 tells us that "endurance builds character, which gives us a hope that will never disappoint us. All of this happens because God has given us the Holy Spirit, who fills our hearts with his love" (CEV).

Let's get into the nitty gritty of working through these things as we consider wanting, worrying, and waiting while God's plan unfolds.

EIGHTEEN

WANTING, WORRYING, AND WAITING

hen you have five kids, you can be sure that someone always wants something: a doll, a game, a video, a new computer program, an album. Often they'll express that *want* like this: "Hey Dad, I need a new . . ."

When I was five years old, I wanted a drum set. Did I need it? No. After I banged on it for a few hours, my parents were pretty sure they didn't want it either! In time, I decided I didn't really want that drum set as much as I thought, and we sold it.

Maybe, like me, you get easily sucked in by the latest gizmos. I have seen a new keyboard or piece of electronic equipment for the recording studio and convinced myself that I had to have it. Did I need it?

Not necessarily. I've done the same thing with albums, videos, clothes, even cars.

As I've matured (and heeded the wise input of my wife), I've grown less impulsive about purchasing things. I'm learning to separate the *wants* from the *needs*.

Our heavenly Father doesn't have a problem in this area. He clearly distinguishes between the two and He "knows the things you have need of before you ask Him" (Matt. 6:8 NKJV).

He knows our needs but still wants us to ask. It reminds us that we are dependent on Him, that He is the One who provides for us each day.

Some people, however, think their relationship with God is similar to Aladdin's power over the genie. Their belief is this: if you want something, tell God to do it for you. Instead of magic words such as *abracadabra*, they like to quote from John 15:7, which says, "Ask any request you like, and it will be granted!" (TLB). It sounds like God is handing us a magic lamp—that is, unless you read the beginning of the verse: "If you stay in me and obey my commands . . ."

That phrase changes everything. It moves us

from what sounds like a blank check for selfishness to a way of filtering our desires through His commands and living in His presence.

If you want something that violates the commandments to love God first or love others as ourselves, look for a warning light flashing in your soul. As our motives or desires are changed, we are changed. And as we are changed, the things we ask for are likely to change as well. The two form a perfect circle to keep us on track.

Psalm 37:3–5 says this: "Trust in the LORD, and do good; / Dwell in the land, and feed on His faithfulness. / Delight yourself also in the LORD, / And He shall give you the desires of your heart. / Commit your way to the LORD, / Trust also in Him, / And He shall bring it to pass" (NKJV).

It's easy to get our cart before the horse, to focus on the desire before we delight ourselves in Him. He pulls us aside, almost as a coach would a player to say, "Let's look at priorities. Number one, who do you trust? I must be first. Get that part right. Fire up your faith so that you'll be receptive to the right desires. As you're doing that, I'll place within you the desires that are best for you." As we do that, we'll want what He wants for our lives.

Some years ago, our pastor encouraged the church to pray this prayer: "Lord, I want to want what You want for me." It's not just a play on words; it's a simple confession of the heart designed to align our desires with His.

Are you open to praying that? I encourage you to try it and see if God doesn't change your priorities, help you discern *wants* from *needs*, and calm your soul.

That calming effect is especially important if you're inclined to worry.

WHEN ANXIETY ATTACKS

I'm thankful that worrying doesn't take up much of my time. I tend to accept things at face value and roll with them. But I know that many struggle with anxiety, so let's think through it.

The root word of worry conveys the idea of being distracted or divided. You can imagine multiple voices questioning in your mind: *What if this happens? What if that happens? How am I going to do this? Who's going to do that?*

In those frantic times, we need to hear Paul's encouraging words to the church at Philippi: "Don't worry about anything, but pray about everything. With thankful hearts offer up your prayers and requests to God. Then, because you belong to Christ Jesus, God will bless you with peace that no one can completely understand. And this peace will control the way you think and feel" (4:6–7 CEV).

Just as Jesus and His disciples seemed destined to go down with their ship until the Master spoke to the stormy waves, we need to hear Him say to our souls: "Peace. Be still!" Even in the throes of trying to discern God's plan, the small voice of the Holy Spirit will whisper comfort to get us through the confusion we face.

But what if answers don't come quickly?

WAITING AND WAITING AND . . .

You've probably heard the prayer, "Lord, give me patience. And give it to me NOW!" Waiting isn't easy. We want to meet deadlines, mark off our accomplishments, and move on.

I learned that with the *Live the Life* album. Originally, we said that it would come out in October 1997, but we weren't happy with it. We figured we'd have it ready by January 1998. When that time came, it still wasn't what we wanted so we moved the date to April. Running nearly six months late, we were all pretty frustrated with our scheduling mishaps, but we were finally pleased with the album. It took patience, but I know that I'm much happier with the record than I would have been if we had hurried things along.

Romans 8:25 in *The Message* offers a great insight for those of us who are addicted to instant gratification. "The longer we wait, the larger we become, and the more joyful our expectancy." We may not know exactly what life holds, but we can be sure that God plans to use us. Instead of growing more frustrated by an uncertain future, is it possible to turn that energy into anticipation?

That's just what my friend, Michael Nolan, did.

A WHIRLWIND ROMANCE?

Michael, who cowrote this book, hoped to one day get married, but years came and went with no serious relationship. When he was thirty-eight, he ran into Nancy, a girl he knew through Susan, a mutual friend. There was enough of a spark in the conversation that he asked her out a few nights later. They had such a good time on their first date, they went out again the following evening.

In only five months, they became engaged and four months later, they were married. Sounds like a whirlwind romance, doesn't it? Then, let me back up.

Michael had first met Nancy eleven years before their first date. He knew Susan because they attended the same church and Susan was in grad school with Nancy. Once or twice a year, Susan brought her two circles of friends together for a party or cookout.

Every year for eleven years, Michael and Nancy had seen each other without any romantic sparks flying. Then suddenly something changed and this one friendly conversation led to a lifetime together.

Now let me back up even further. Fourteen years before their first date, Michael had written in his journal what he hoped to find in a wife. When he proposed to Nancy, he read this and said, "It's taken fourteen years for God to design and deliver the kind of woman I need. And it's taken me fourteen years of change to be ready to receive you into my life."

How would you answer this question: was this romance fast-paced or unbelievably slow? It depends on how you look at it.

That's true of so many things in our lives. When I was a kid, it seemed to take forever for Christmas to finally come. The month of December crawled by, then the twenty-fifth came and went in the blink of an eye.

Now years blaze by with blinding speed. It seems like only yesterday that our older son, Ryan, was born. Now he's in high school and, in no time, he'll be out on his own.

Waiting is often a matter of perspective. If you want to make a call and someone else is using the phone, two minutes can seem like an eternity. But if you're properly focused, the waiting may not seem so excruciating.

In *My Utmost for His Highest*, Oswald Chambers offers these words: "There are times when you can't understand why you cannot do what you want to do. When God brings a time of waiting, and appears to be unresponsive, don't fill it with busyness, just wait. The time of waiting may come to teach you the meaning of sanctification—to be set apart from sin and made holy—or it may come after the process of sanctification has begun to teach you what service means. Never run before God gives you His direction. If you have the slightest doubt, then He is not guiding. Whenever there is doubt—wait."[2]

What do we do when we find ourselves in that place of wanting, worrying, and waiting? We would do well to follow the apostle Paul's example.

TO KNOW CONTENTMENT

Paul lived a life marked by unpredictability. He went from being a highly regarded persecutor of Christians to a prolific defender of the faith. He was heralded as a great teacher in some cities and tossed into prison in others because he preached about Jesus. He described this up-and-down life in Philippians 4:11–13:

> I have learned to be satisfied with whatever I have. I know what it is to be poor or to have plenty, and I have lived under all kinds of conditions. I know what it means to be full or to be hungry, to have too much or too little. Christ gives me the strength to face anything. (CEV)

Is it wrong to want a girlfriend or boyfriend? Definitely not. Is it wrong to want to be accepted into a particular school? Probably not. Is it wrong to want to get married? No. Should you hope that bad situations turn around for your friends and family? Absolutely.

Christ will give you the strength to hang in there no matter what. He's also there to sustain you through good times as well, times when you imagine the possibilities your life may hold.

NINETEEN

PURSUIT OF
THE DREAM

ne thing you can say for sure about my manager, Michael Blanton: the guy has big dreams.

Sometimes we'll sit around and brainstorm possibilities and just go nuts thinking about things. In our early days together, we were long on enthusiasm and maybe a little short on realism. When he and his partner, Dan Harrell, were first getting their management company off the ground, Amy and I were their only clients. We got excited about mainstream success and thought we'd make it on pop radio in a year. Man, were we naïve!

It took years of building relationships and improving our craft before we were ready to take on the big world of pop music. Through years in Christian music, we learned so much that helped ground us when our opportunities to cross over finally came. Without them, we would have been much less mature and much more likely to make huge mistakes.

When things didn't click immediately, were we disappointed? Yeah, I'd say that we were a little bummed, but now I know that God's timetable was exactly right.

Michael Blanton has spent a great deal of time considering what God's plan means, and I want to pass along his wisdom:

> The first thing you need to know is that God is not a teaser. He doesn't plant dreams inside you so you can crash and burn. They're there for a reason.

When Michael completed his studies at Abilene Christian University, he hoped to start a Christian ski lodge. Instead of moving to the mountains of Colorado upon graduation, the door opened for him to work in Nashville with Belmont Church's youth ministry.

After a year-and-a-half, he tried to get a job in

Christian music but was turned down. He moved back to Abilene and got a job at the chamber of commerce.

A year later Word Records called out of the blue and invited him to come on staff as an A&R (artist and repetoire) director. He was assigned a new artist named Amy Grant (who had been in his youth group) and David Meece.

Both of their careers skyrocketed under Michael's direction, and suddenly he found his services in demand. In time, he left Word to cofound Blanton-Harrell and Reunion Records. Today he codirects Idea Entertainment, which includes Word Records, Pandora Films, and Blanton-Harrell Entertainment.

What has he learned along the way? "Take whatever God has put in your hand today and do something with it," he said. "Be great wherever God puts you—whether you're flipping burgers at McDonalds or selling stereos at Circuit City or stocking the shelves at Home Depot.

"Don't worry about that huge thing that you want to attain. God is big enough to get you there in His timing."

Dreams and Decisions

When I first met with Michael back in 1981, I played him "You Need A Savior" and "The Race Is On." He told me to bring in ten or twelve more songs of that quality. I was so eager to make things happen that I was back in his office three weeks later with many of the songs that I ultimately recorded.

One of them was "Friends," which Michael instantly knew would connect with listeners. But it presented a problem for him. Should the song be given to Amy for her upcoming project or held until I had the opportunity to record my own album?

I guess you know that the answer fell somewhere in the middle. I recorded it for *Michael W. Smith Project* as a duet with Amy and, as Michael predicted, it remains my most popular song.

"So many of the decisions that any of us make may seem insignificant, but they matter over time," he reflected. "You just don't know how God's plan is going to work itself out."

One of his key responsibilities in working with me was to help me take a good look at where I was going. "Your gifting is different than your dream," he told me one day. "You're going to have an impact on the world, but I don't think pop music is going to be the primary way." From listening to the way my music encouraged Christians, he knew that my main audience would always be believers—and that's fine by me.

I needed some time to think that through and allow God to refine the vision that He had for me. Almost all of our dreams require a bit of fine-tuning. Some people, however, seem resistant to that.

About a year ago, two guys I know moved to Nashville hoping to get recording contracts. One worked as a waiter to make ends meet while the other focused exclusively on music.

The former is still plugging away, writing in his free time and optimistic that his dream will one day be fulfilled. The latter got frustrated after only a few months and moved away, bitter and angry. The most important advice I give anyone who asks me about a career in music is: carefully count the costs *before* you take a leap of faith.

Michael Blanton agrees: "People are not quick to embrace their own situations. They get caught up with where they want to end up, instead of seeing where they are now and doing what is necessary to move forward.

"God will either fulfill the dream or change the dream over time," he added. "So many times the dream will change—and that's good. One person may need to focus; another may need to spread out.

"I find myself asking: 'What are the other pieces that go with that dream?' Maybe you start out thinking you want to be a singer but what you come to find out is that you're really a background vocalist or a choir director or a manager."

By the way, your dreams don't have to be big and dramatic. If God plants in your heart a desire to help with the music program at your local church, please recognize what a valuable service you are rendering and how much that obedience honors Him.

I love performing in concerts but some of my favorite times at the keyboard have been playing old hymns at the house when we host praise gatherings for friends and family members. There is beauty in the simplicity of it all and it's so much easier to keep the focus on the Lord in times like these.

FOR ALL YOU NON-MUSICAL FOLKS

I've used music examples here because that's what people ask about the most. But you can apply the principles to any dreams you may hold.

Whatever your dream, place it in your hands and offer it to God. If you're afraid that He will snatch it from you, it's time to do some real soul-searching. You might need the help of a friend or mentor to sort through your feelings.

In fact, it's a good idea to talk to a number of people about your dreams, especially people from different walks of life. Adding their perspectives will add to your total perspective. Heed the wisdom of Proverbs 15:22: "Plans fail for lack of counsel, but with many advisers they succeed" (NIV).

And by all means, count the cost before making any commitment. Move closer to your dreams with your eyes wide open.

In concluding this chapter, some of the lyrics from "Pursuit of the Dream" seem appropriate:

> *It's alright to find yourself*
> *Thinking now and then*

About the way you want your life to be
Anticipating what lies
Just around the bend
Can't wait to see

Comes the times of decision
Some you dodge and some you should face
As you see the big picture
There will be some dues to pay

Break down the barriers but
Don't bend the rules
Never forget your roots
As you head for something new
Ride thru the shades of desire
Letting the light be seen
And He'll steer your heart in the
Pursuit of the dream [1]

I pray that you'll stay on course with your plans, but in case you've drifted, it's good to know that our gracious heavenly Father often provides an alternative to save us from despair.

TWENTY

PLAN B
AND BEYOND

ometimes something may seem like a good idea at the time but may later prove otherwise. Take my hairstyles over the years as a prime example. If I look through my old album covers and press photos, I cringe—and then I laugh.

If you've seen them, you know what I'm talking about. I've had bad bangs and mousse overkill—and my Caesar cut wasn't a big hit with anybody.

What I thought was right at the moment definitely wasn't in the long run. Obviously something as insignificant as a haircut rarely has a permanent effect on a person's life but this principle bears considerably more weight in other areas.

Let me share a story with you offered by Pastor Don Finto. Some years ago, he counseled a woman who is a respected Christian leader, the head of a ministry that touched a number of cities. Without going into unnecessary details, she began dating a man who wasn't a Christian. At the time, she thought he was everything she hoped for in a husband, her plan A. Things changed suddenly after their relationship led to a one-night sexual encounter.

Almost immediately she realized what all her friends had been trying to tell her: this man was drawing her away from God. She quickly went to Don who listened as she recounted her story and confessed her sin.

"Do you think I should resign?" she asked him, fully willing to submit to his counsel. "I don't want this to destroy all that God has done through this ministry."

Don prayed for guidance and then said to her, "You could step down, but I think for you that would mean Satan has gained a greater victory."

You see, the enemy always wants to sabotage God's plan for our lives. He hits us in our weak spots and wears us down with his almost relentless prodding.

"Living in complete purity was God's plan A for you, but we're not at that place anymore," Don said to her with great tenderness. "Now the thing to do is to discern His plan B. You've allowed some misery to come into your life, but you've got to find a way for God to use it, for Him to turn this defeat into victory."

Because of this experience, the woman came to a place of fresh compassion in her ministry. She cared for people in a way that she never had before and found this spiritual wound actually prepared her for God's healing. Instead of being devastated, she allowed God to raise her up to walk in Him more closely, His plan B.

Don would want me to tell you that he wouldn't necessarily give the same counsel to another person in a similar situation, but it seemed to be the Lord's will for this individual. The principle remains the same regardless of who he might be counseling: how can God gain a victory from what Satan intended to use to bring about defeat?

Sometimes it feels like we miss God's best for our lives. It's like we were supposed to catch a plane at 6:45 and we arrive at the airport at 7:00. We feel stranded, unsure of where to go or what to do next.

The Lord sometimes allows us a second chance, a special kind of grace, to get back to plan A. Those who have been sexually active and then sign up for the True Love Waits campaign understand it completely. The organization offers its pledge for those who want become secondary virgins, to have the opportunity to start over spiritually and emotionally.

Sometimes an opportunity you thought you missed will come around again—often to your great surprise.

For some who reject God's plan A for their lives, the consequences of their actions can be devastating. One of the most painful feelings is regret. But with God's mercy, we don't have to remain crippled by its weight.

The Message drives home this idea with its powerful paraphrase of 2 Corinthians 7:10: "Distress that drives us to God . . . turns us around. It gets us back in the way of salvation. We never regret that kind of pain."

THE VIEW GROWS CLEARER

Sometimes plan B isn't developed as a result of sin. Sometimes it's just that we don't always hear God clearly. First Corinthians 13:9–10, 12 speaks to this: "For we know in part and we prophesy in part. But when that which is perfect has come, then that which is in part will be done away . . . For now we see in a mirror, dimly, but then face to face. Now I know in part, but then I shall know just as I also am known" (NKJV).

We're definitely not living in perfection right now. Often we strain to hear God speaking and don't hear anything at all. Hopefully, we're a little more mature than yesterday but still not to the place where we always discern God's plan for our lives.

Pastor Don Finto suggests that this is an ongoing process. "The tighter we walk with the Lord, the more specific His plans become to us," he said. He believes that Psalm 25:8–9, 12–14 speaks clearly to how our relationship with God affects our ability to discern the right path.

> Good and upright is the LORD;
>   therefore he instructs sinners
>   in his ways.
> He guides the humble in what is right

and teaches them his way . . .
Who, then, is the man that fears the
    LORD?
    He will instruct him in the way
        chosen for him.
He will spend his days in prosperity,
    and his descendants will inherit the
        land.
The LORD confides in those who fear him;
    he makes his covenant known to
        them. (NIV)

Rocketown's plan A and plan B are related but different. So it is with many of the things we undertake. We have an ideal plan laid out but something goes awry, and we must figure out where to go from there.

A few years ago I got a letter from a young woman who entered college as a premed major. The intensity of her studies increased until it absolutely overwhelmed her.

"I no longer had the desire to learn or the energy to keep putting on a front concerning who I was," she wrote. "I was also overcome by an immense fear of failure to the point where I would avoid doing something altogether if there was even the slightest chance I'd be less than the best at it."

She graduated with a 4.0 grade point average but was completely disillusioned. Instead of going on to medical school, she took a job as a waitress.

In her letter, she said that my music spoke to her during those troubled times. "Place in This World" was especially meaningful as she considered what to do with the rest of her life.

"To make a long story shorter," she concluded, "I scored well on my MCAT (medical college admissions test) practice test, and I'll start medical school this fall."

Perhaps God's plan A was for her to be better grounded before beginning her studies. Or maybe her plan A required going through tough times to mature her. I do know that she is moving forward with an excitement and enthusiasm she didn't have previously.

You may find some areas in your life where you've gone through plans C through Y in search of what's right. I know that God will be right there even if it takes until plan Z to get you where you should be.

If God was prone to giving up on people, He would surely have left the Israelites stranded in the wilderness, because they constantly complained and disobeyed. He didn't. He brought them to the promised land just as He said He would.

No matter how frustrated you may be with the detours and dead ends you've taken, here's something you have to believe with all your heart: "He who has begun a good work in you will complete it until the day of Jesus Christ" (Phil. 1:6 NKJV).

Let's look at the final applications of the markers in this book—place, purpose, passion, and plan—for your life as we draw our thoughts to a conclusion.

TWENTY ONE

YOUR PLACE IN THIS WORLD

 ew Scriptures are more exciting than the words found in Jeremiah 29:11: "'For I know the plans I have for you,' declares the LORD, 'plans to prosper you and not to harm you, plans to give you hope and a future'" (NIV).

What is hope? It's longing for something with a sense of expectation. It's that unstoppable belief that good will come and that obstacles will not triumph. It's having confidence that even when things look bleak, there's always reason to believe that things will turn out for the good.

I join the writer of Romans in offering this blessing for you: "Now may the God of hope fill you will all joy and peace in believing, that you may abound in hope by the power of the Holy Spirit" (15:13 NKJV).

As hope flows into your life, it makes the future a little easier to face. Yes, there are uncertainties and questions and a thousand "what if" scenarios. I don't honestly know how many details of life are in God's journal for each of us. I'll leave that for the theologians and scholars to debate.

I do know that God is true to His Word, and He has shown Himself faithful to His people time after time. David praised Him saying, "You, LORD God, have done many wonderful things, / and you have planned marvelous things for us. / No one is like you! / I would never be able to tell all you have done" (Ps. 40:5 CEV).

What Can You Know About Your Place in This World?

To help you get a handle on this question, allow me pass along some counsel from Pastor Don Finto. "We don't start out as blank slates," he explained. "Each of us comes into this world wired differently, and we can't change our wiring. We cannot become something we weren't destined to become. Jacob couldn't become Esau."

But obviously that leaves a lot of room for possibilities. Don continued, "I can only get out what God has put in me." Some of those things may be hidden—gifts so buried that we don't discover them for years.

Here are a few suggestions as you try to discern God's plan for your life:

Discover your gifts. Some people are natural-born athletes. Others are brilliant in math. A few of us, though not me, are electronic wizards. What are you good at? The answers may be helpful as you think about what you might want to do for a living.

See what the Bible has to say about gifts as well. Look up the lists given in Romans 12:4–8, 1 Corinthians 12:27–31, and Ephesians 4:11–12. You'll read about everything from leadership to healing in these scriptures. The really exciting part is that your place in this world is in there somewhere. Crack open your Bible and let God speak to you through these passages.

Consider what has proven right. Can you

look back over time and see events in your life that were unquestionably part of God's plan for you—a class you took, an experience you had, a job you liked, a quality in a relationship that you found essential?

Take note of these things. Ask why they are so meaningful to you. Is there something about these memories from the past that you should look for in your future?

Spend time in quiet. That's not the same as a quiet time where you pray, read Scripture, and perhaps write in a journal. Just focus on the Lord and wait silently for Him to direct your mind.

Pastor Don Finto told of a teenager who was a model Christian in his church. He always sat on the front row, participated in every event, and even attended a Christian college. Years passed and Don learned that the man was arrested for robbery. Don visited him and asked what caused him to veer off course. "I never allowed myself to think," he responded. "I surrounded myself with friends, music, noise. I knew if I was quiet I would have to deal with mistakes I was making."

In the quiet, you may find sin exposed as well as guidance that will encourage you on your journey.

Listen to those you trust. Proverbs 20:5 says: "The purposes of a man's heart are deep waters, / but a man of understanding draws them out" (NIV). Invite people who know you well and whose judgment you trust to help you draw out your thoughts.

Ask them to talk with you about your strengths and weaknesses. Weigh their words carefully and prayerfully. Their perspectives could be tremendously helpful as you try to get a better picture of God's plan for your life.

Whenever possible, test-drive your options. Before you choose a school, spend a weekend there. Take a class in a subject that is related to the career you are considering to see if you like it. Sign up for a short-term missions program before you commit to a two-year "tour of duty."

Walk through a neighborhood that you're considering making your home. Spend time conversing with married couples if you're dating someone seriously and think it may lead to marriage. These are simple, practical ways to "count the cost" before making a commitment that you may later regret.

Keep growing closer to God. Don thinks that the tighter we walk with the Lord, the more specific direction we receive. I have to agree. The times I hear from God most clearly are either when my heart is closely tuned to Him or when I am most desperate.

There's great wisdom in David's prayer recorded in Psalm 119:133: "Direct my footsteps according to your word; / let no sin rule over me" (NIV).

As we fortify our faith with more of His Word living inside us, we have instant access to godly counsel. Bible verses pop from our memory to give us direction to face the situation at hand. The more of God's Word we input, the more situations we're ready to encounter.

Instead of allowing sin to sit in the driver's seat and steer our lives, we kick it out of the car and allow God to help us navigate. When sin and its effects are lessened, our lives become less complicated, more peaceful. With less static on the line, it's easier to hear the voice of the Lord.

Finally, live under grace daily. Mark my words: you will make mistakes. You will have a knot in your stomach that tells you that you've missed God's plan A at least a few times in your life. Instead of dwelling on that fact or beating yourself up, allow yourself to be blown away once again by God's amazing graciousness toward us.

I hope this book has stirred useful thinking within you. I hope you can more easily identify your place in this world, that you see your purpose with greater clarity, that you've refired the passion for living life to its fullest, and that you have a greater understanding of God's plan for you.

As a benediction for our journey together, I offer this prayer from Hebrews 13:20–21: "Now may the God of peace who brought up our Lord Jesus from the dead, that great Shepherd of the sheep, through the blood of the everlasting covenant, make you complete in every good work to do His will, working in you what is well pleasing in His sight, through Jesus Christ, to whom be glory forever and ever. Amen" (NKJV).

Notes

Chapter 1

1. "Place in This World." Written by Michael W. Smith, Wayne Kirkpatrick, and Amy Grant. © 1990 Milene Music, Inc. (ASCAP), Careers-BMG Music Publishing, Inc. (BMI), and Age to Age Music, Inc. (ASCAP). International rights secured. All rights reserved. Used by permission.

Chapter 3

1. "Give It Away." Written by Michael W. Smith, Wayne Kirkpatrick, and Amy Grant. © 1992 Milene Music, Inc. (ASCAP), Careers-BMG Music Publishing, Inc. (BMI), Magic Beans Music (BMI), and Age to Age Music, Inc. (ASCAP). All rights on behalf of Magic Beans Music administered by Careers-BMG. International rights secured. All rights reserved. Used by permission.

Chapter 4

1. "Emily." Written by Michael W. Smith and Wayne Kirkpatrick. © 1987 (renewed 1995) Milene Music, Inc. (ASCAP), Careers-BMG Music Publishing, Inc. (BMI). International rights secured. All rights reserved. Used by permission.

Chapter 8

1. "Secret Ambition." Written by Michael W. Smith, Wayne Kirkpatrick, and Amy Grant © 1988 (renewed 1998) Milene Music, Inc. (ASCAP), Careers-BMG Music Publishing, Inc. (BMI) and Riverstone Music, Inc. (ASCAP). International rights secured. All rights reserved. Used by permission.

2. Oswald Chambers, *My Utmost for His Highest*. (Grand Rapids, Discovery House, 1995), January 4.

3. "Live the Life." Written by Michael W. Smith and Brent Bourgeois. © 1997 Milene Music, Inc. (ASCAP), Deer Valley Music (ASCAP), W.B.M. Music Corp. (SESAC), ADC Music (SESAC), and Edinburgh Songs (SESAC). All rights on behalf of ADC Music and Edinburgh Songs administered by W.B.M. Music. International rights secured. All rights reserved. Used by permission.

4. Reuben Welch, *We Really Do Need Each Other*. (Grand Rapids: Zondervan, 1973), 72.

Chapter 14

1. "I Miss the Way." Written by Michael W. Smith and Wayne Kirkpatrick. © 1988 (renewed 1998) Milene Music, Inc. (ASCAP) and Carrers-BMG Music Publishing, Inc. (BMI). International rights secured. All rights reserved. Used by permission.

2. "Missing Person." Written by Michael W. Smith and Wayne Kirkpatrick. © 1998 Milene Music, Inc. (ASCAP), Deer Valley Music (ASCAP), Warner-Tamerlane Publishing Corp. (BMI), and Sell the Cow Music (BMI). All rights on behalf of Sell the Cow Music administered by Warner-Tamerlane. International rights secured. All rights reserved. Used by permission.

Chapter 15

1. Tim Hansel, *Holy Sweat*. (Dallas: Word Books, 1987), 73.

Chapter 18

1. Oswald Chambers, *My Utmost for His Highest*. (Grand Rapids, Discovery House, 1995), January 1.

Chapter 20

1. "Pursuit of the Dream." Written by Michael W. Smith and Wayne Kirkpatrick. © 1985 Milene Music, Inc. (ASCAP), Careers-BMG Music Publishing, Inc. (BMI), and Magic Beans Music (BMI). All rights on behalf of Magic Beans Music administered by Careers-BMG. International rights secured. All rights reserved. Used by permission.